More Advance Praise

I read *Take Heart!* while flying home after a speaking engagement. I was tired and definitely cranky. Nevertheless, I did not put this book down until I finished it, and I laughed and cried and laughed again all the way home!

— Lola Gillebaard, humorist and author of *Laughter Made From Experience*

After my open-heart surgery I was feeling pretty miserable. Then I read *Take Heart!* and I laughed so hard I was able to see my circumstances through different eyes. I couldn't wait to tell my sister to read it.

— Lucy Vitale, open-heart surgery patient

You will be deeply touched by Rudy's courage and quirky sense of humor. Her journey is a powerful lesson to us all on how to view the glass half full and to celebrate each moment of life. Rudy's life is a testimonial to rising above obstacles and finding peace and joy in whatever circumstance life may bring.

— Barbara Glanz, CSP, author of *Balancing Acts*, *Handle with CARE* and *CARE Packages for the Workplace*

Curl up in your favorite chair with this book and prepare to be heartwarmed. Galdonik's stories remind us of the miracle of living and loving and laughing.

— Mary LoVerde, author of *I Used to Have a Handle on Life But It Broke*

Rudy's *Take Heart!* tickles the funny bone while lifting the spirit. Her stories will touch your heart and inspire your faith. My life is richer for having read her journey.

— Lucy Hedrick, author of *Get Organized in the Digital Age*

Take Heart!

True Stories of Life, Love, and Laughter

Rudy Wilson Galdonik

Broad Horizons Press

Author's Note

Names of some people have been changed
due primarily to the constraints of the menopausal mind . . .
I just can't remember them.

Copyright © 2004 by Rudy Wilson Galdonik.
All rights reserved.
Printed in the United States of America.
No part of this book may be used or reproduced
in any manner whatsoever without
written permission except in the case of
brief quotations embodied in
critical articles and reviews.
For information, please contact
Broad Horizons Press, PO Box 528,
East Greenwich, RI 02818.

This book is meant only to entertain. Any slights of people
or organizations are unintentional. If professional advice or
other expert assistance is required, the services of a competent
professional person should be sought.

Excerpt from *The Positive Power of Jesus Christ* by Norman
Vincent Peale. Copyright © 1980 by Norman Vincent Peale.
Reprinted by permission of Tyndale House Publishers, Inc.,
Carol Stream, Illinois.

Cover design and interior layout by Karen Saunders

First Edition

Library of Congress Cataloging-in-Publication Data

Wilson Galdonik, Rudy.
Take Heart! True Stories of Life, Love, and Laughter – 1st ed.
p.cm.
ISBN 0-9741852-4-8
Library of Congress Control Number: 2003094344

*A cheerful heart is good medicine
but a crushed spirit dries up the bones.*

— Proverbs 17:22

* * *

Many thanks to the countless nurses
and medical caregivers
whose names I will never know
but whose gentle touch I will never forget.
You saw me as a person, not a specimen.
You encouraged me to laugh
when the world said nothing was funny.
You showed me compassion
when I was my most ornery.

It takes a very special person
to devote a lifetime to caring for others.
Thank you for being who you are
and doing what you do.

And to
Darah, Brad, and Mike

I love you with all my heart,
broken and damaged though it may be.

Contents

Foreword ix

Preface xiii

And the *Thump-psssh* Goes On 1

One Step at a Time 11

Morphing from "Doris" to "Scar Chest" 21

Diagnosis: Black Lab Nut 55

Icing on the Cake 71

Once a Yankee, Always a Yankee 81

To Trust a Clever Canary 93

This Must Be Love 105

Hunk-A Hunk-A Burning Love 123

Three's a Crowd 131

Emily 149

Garbage Envy 171

Foreword

Ability to find and use humor in life doesn't appear on any doctor's annual physical form. It doesn't show up on a CAT scan or a blood test. But I am certain that it's important. Patients who have this characteristic get better faster, have fewer complications, and are happier. Those who are particularly gifted in this category can transfer some of it to others and in doing so make people happier and healthier. They make great friends and usually have great friendships. Medical science acknowledges that this makes for a healthier life. Rudy Galdonik gets an A-plus in this category.

I spent a fair bit of my day yesterday laughing as I read this book. But there was nothing funny about my first encounter with Rudy Galdonik. As she recounts in "Three's A Crowd," I happened to be in my office late on a stormy winter Friday night when her echocardiogram test was completed. This earned me the privilege of telling a skeptical patient I had never met that she had a serious infection in her heart, and that instead of going home she must proceed to a hospital bed via a crowded emergency room.

As you will see, Rudy's initial reaction to any new physician can be summarized in one word: *suspicion*. So things didn't exactly get off on the best foot between Rudy and me. To her credit, Rudy got over it. This was not the first time Rudy had been presented with unexpected seriously bad news in her life. Among the stories here are a number of similar experiences. But this book isn't really about Rudy's encounters with the unfairness of life. It's about an unfailing spirit and an ability to find humor in the midst of life's nasty tricks.

Rudy's keen wit distills the comedy out of situations that might seem only tragic, and she uses the humor to deal with the unavoidable adversities. In doing so she not only manages to triumph personally, she also lifts up others – family, friends, chance acquaintances, even her physicians – who are fortunate enough to be around her. If you are lucky enough to pick up this book and read it, she will have that effect on you.

You will see that Rudy Galdonik is not a passive passenger. She uses the humor she finds in her personal setbacks to move forward, and you get the opportunity to laugh about it here. But Rudy also gives back in other ways that she does not write about in this book. She barely mentions the time she devotes to building housing for strangers trapped in the grip of poverty in Mexico. Rudy also volunteers her time making important contributions to the local chapter of the American Heart Association. And when her heart surgeon identifies patients who are having a particularly difficult time coping, he calls on Rudy to encourage them. It would be wrong to portray her as a Mother Teresa. She is too irreverent and way too funny. But finding the humor in life somehow helps give her the energy to help others. This book is just one more way that Rudy Galdonik has found to give back. Congratulations on finding it.

— Alan J. Shurman M.D., FACC,
University Cardiology Foundation

Preface

In September 2000, my 16-year-old son Brad announced that he wanted to hike the Appalachian Trail. Nice idea. A lame-brain idea, the kind teenagers have a tendency to produce, but nice idea, nonetheless.

"Sure, someday," was my response.

"No, I want to hike it this year," he insisted. That's when my mothering instincts kicked in. I blasted the kid. I reminded him he was only a kid. He had never spent one night alone in the woods, and he still had two years left before he even graduated from *high school*. And he was expecting me to give him permission to hike from Georgia to Maine, *alone*? I squished those plans like a bug on a busy city street.

Then in the heat of the moment, I threw in a comment that I believed was a surefire reinforcement for my refusal to buy into this craziness. "However, if *God* wants you to hike the trail, and He makes it all happen, and He gives me a peace about it, then who am I to stop you?" There. Done deal.

Eleven months later, on August 14, 2001, Brad reached the summit of Katahdin in Maine after hiking 2,168 miles, alone. So much for my plan of keeping the kid safely tucked away at home.

As Brad's hike started, family and friends urged, "Keep us informed. Let us know how it's going with him." So I gathered names and I began sending out e-mail updates. To my surprise, after every update more friends and even strangers asked to be included in this adventure via the miracle of cyberspace. People from as far away as Australia kept abreast of my son's hike. I was having a blast writing about *hiker's stink*, bears dropping from trees, and all the things that Brad was experiencing on the trail. I shared it all vicariously while sitting at my computer. I was almost sad when I wrote my last update detailing my son's success. It had been quite a journey for both of us.

Then one month later, I was visiting with friends, Lou and Jonellen Heckler. Jonellen, a novelist with five books and numerous translations to her credit, said something that became the catalyst for this book. She said, "Rudy, every writer has a voice. And that voice is unique to them, and until you recognize and honor that voice, you'll never be successful in writing." That statement struck me at my core. Until then I had dabbled in speaking and writing in corporate settings. But it was hard work, and my successes were few.

Before Brad's hike, I made numerous attempts to add my contribution to the mountain of existing self-help and how-to books. The prospect of writing a book was huge. As I explored different topics, a little voice in my head would whisper, *Are you NUTS? Who are you trying to kid? You can't possibly write a self-help book. You NEED help yourself.*

But then I looked back at my writing while Brad was on the trail. Brad embraced the impossible and made it his own. I wrote funny and had fun at the same time. Brad showed me how to think big and not stop at impossible odds. Jonellen gave me permission to let the funny out. In addition, a key factor in my faith had been my eventual realization that faith and funny go together.

I now believe Jonellen's comment goes way beyond my writing. I believe we each have a voice, a purpose for being. When we recognize and honor that purpose, we will be living our lives as God intended, and success will naturally follow. As you read these essays I hope you see yourself in the funny stuff. I hope you will look at your own life and ask yourself if you are truly living your purpose. I hope you will begin to cast off restrictions on your thinking and at the same time, if faith is not a part of your life, to consider the possibility of a power greater than you. You will be amazed at all the good things that await you. I promise.

And the *Thump-psssh* Goes On

One of my favorite childhood memories involves one of my parents suggesting, "Hey, anybody want to go for a drive?" At a time when gasoline hovered at a steady 30 cents a gallon, this was the perfect pastime for a family that didn't have any money but did have one kid who was a heart patient. Cheap and sedentary, this activity was far better than mountain climbing, yacht racing or other more expensive and physically challenging options.

My heart condition was discovered during my kindergarten exam. A doctor placed a stethoscope to my chest, and instead of the normal *thump-thump, thump-thump* sound, he heard *thump-psssh, thump-psssh*. I had been born with a hole in my heart. So what do you do with a kid who has a hole in her heart when open-heart surgery is in its infancy? You devise all means of creative, sedentary activities to give the appearance that she is living a full, active life. And if you're lucky, she'll be dumb enough to think so, too. My parents were very lucky people.

It was decided that I could bide my time with music. A variety of potential instruments was considered. The tuba or a set of drums was out of the question as they would be too heavy for the tiny heart patient or too nerve-wracking for the temperamental father. So with the help of an aunt and uncle, a piano was purchased. Its gleaming keys and massive presence in our tiny living room suggested that great music would fill our home. Instead, scales (poorly executed) and *Chopsticks* were all I could produce.

Not willing to give up on music so quickly, my parents decided the flute was a better option. So a flute was rented and a chair was selected. I was to spend my life sitting and playing the sweet-sounding tunes of the flute. There were only two problems: I didn't have an ounce of interest and skill when it came to anything musical, and the flute, when played correctly, plugs up the mouth, rendering the player unable to speak. And, for me, speaking was synonymous with breathing; it was what got me into trouble; it was my life. The flute showed much more promise as a weapon. With a simple flick of the wrist I could clunk my sister, Chris, whenever circumstances warranted it. And then, if my mother heard commotion, I could just as quickly return the flute to my mouth and assume the angelic look of a heart patient diligently practicing her craft.

About this time, kids in the neighborhood took to roller-skating. This seemed like fun, but the physical exertion presented a problem. Finally, not wanting their daughters to be left out, my parents purchased one pair of roller skates and announced that my sister and I could share. I got the left one, Chris took the right. Hitting the sidewalks on one skate slowed us down tremendously, enough for people who drove by to roll down the window and yell, "Hey, stupid! Don't you know you're supposed to use two skates?" It was the first example of the discrimination I experienced as a kid who was different, not to mention the fact that my sister began to realize she was regularly being sucked into arrangements specifically tailored to keep me sedentary. This did not make for a happy sister. It did, however, lead to many necessary additional clunkings of the flute to keep her attitude in check.

When it came time for swimming lessons, my Mom enrolled me just like the normal kids, but as each session began, she would quietly whisper in the lifeguard's ear. At the end of those conversations the swim instructor's eyes would lock onto mine with a silent message: *Ohhh, I see. Yes, I'll be careful.* As the lessons progressed, we kids would regularly line up at the edge of the pool waiting our turn to demonstrate our newly mastered strokes. Whenever it came to my turn, I would push off, fully expecting to streak through the water with the skill and promise of a potential Olympian. Instead, after my third or fourth kick or pull of the arms the lifeguard would start clapping, thanking me with way too much enthusiasm for my effort. I was still in water up to my knees and I was already done. It didn't take long for my fellow swimmates to hate the fact that I could somehow excel in this class without even getting my face wet.

All this helped fuel my love of car rides. Going for a drive was far from an ordinary outing, even though the ultimate destination would be the same driveway from which we had left. No, this drive had a name: it was a *Looking in People's Houses* drive. Not to be confused with a *Looking AT People's Houses*, this activity had to be performed in the evenings so household lights could best illuminate what we were spying on. At Christmas time this activity could be slightly altered to a *Looking at People's Lights* drive. Occasionally, my family would find itself in the car at night with an actual purpose – we had someplace to go – and it was only a matter of time before some member of my highly creative clan would pipe in with, "Hey, why don't we look in people's houses?" Those evenings counted as both exciting *and* productive.

On those special evenings, my family would board our 1950s Ford that looked like a Mallomar on wheels, and my sister and I would bounce around in the back seat, pressing our noses against the glass as we *oohed* and *aahed* at the houses we passed. My father's sole responsibility was to navigate us slowly through neighborhoods far and wide, eyes on the road, hands at the wheel in the 10 and 2 o'clock position. My mother, who was also seated in the front, had a special role. She had the advantage of being taller in addition to older and wiser than us kids, so her assignment was to call out particularly interesting sights that we were about to pass. "Oh, look at that! See how pretty that living room is," or perhaps, "Can you believe the color of those walls? My, my." I have often thought that if our family included a son, he would have grown up to be an interior designer named Bruce.

If, on occasion, a car ride was the pastime of choice but conditions did not enable a *Looking in People's Houses* drive, (i.e., it was daylight, thereby rendering interiors ineligible for examination) an alternative drive would be employed. A *Let's Get Lost* drive added the thrill of realizing that, if done correctly, my entire family might never be seen again. What my parents didn't realize was that during these very same drives my fragile heart would pound wildly as my entire family would squeal, "Oh, my God, I *really* don't have a *clue* where we are now." As I look back on the adrenaline rush of all this, I suspect that we may have never even left the confines of our small town. Yet, perhaps I am wrong. My parents in their retirement years always insisted on well-orchestrated, highly scheduled, well-supervised packaged tours for vacations, which may have been a direct result of their own adrenaline rush and sense of being out of control while behind the wheel.

My eccentric aunt, never to be outdone, devised her own car ride with us kids that matched her need to live life a touch over the top. Whenever our small town's volunteer fire department would blow its whistle, she would come racing to our curb with the same dedication and focus as the volunteer firefighters. Time was of the essence as my sister and I jumped in the back of her Thunderbird for a *Let's Chase the Fire Trucks* ride. Of course, as luck would have it, the only two fires in the history of my town, when something actually burned down, happened while we were fast asleep in our beds and while we were out of town looking in people's houses.

During these times of exploration, dreams were forming in my young mind. While my mother would point out features such as lighting fixtures and window treatments in other people's houses, the look that took my breath away was rooms filled with books, accented by a fireplace. A love of books had been woven into me, and reading and writing were not a bad option for a heart patient.

I decided to write. Filled with passion, I spun a tale of a little girl moving to a new house; it was to be The Great American Novel. Unfortunately, I didn't understand the concept *write what you know*. I had never moved. I didn't even know anyone else who had ever moved, but I had a pencil, paper, and passion and that seemed sufficient. The first three pages itemized all the possessions the little girl packed in a box. A riveting exposé it was not. By page 4, even I was bored, and this masterpiece was eventually thrown out, along with my extensive airline throw-up bag collection, courtesy of my overzealous Mom, who had her own passion for housecleaning.

Next, I dabbled in poetry. It seemed to me that the most highly regarded poems were always a bit "off," like strawberry milk or Uncle Jules when he was fueled by a fifth of vodka. So in keeping with that perspective, I decided for my first poem to don the persona of an old black man. After reading my poem, Miss McKadin, my third-grade teacher, summoned me to the front of the room. Her crooked finger jabbing toward my face, she pointed out quite emphatically that I was a little girl with blonde pigtails. Possessing no sense of imagination whatsoever, Miss McKadin squashed in an instant any aspirations to become a poet.

In sixth grade I was more successful – I won a writing contest. My story about a ghost got me a whole day out of class to present my winning selection to the entire first grade on Halloween. In the seventh grade, my English teacher told me I *had* to write. I had a gift. This woman, a writer herself, looked like a prune mounted on two toothpicks for legs. And she was telling me I needed to be just like her. One look and the decision was made: writing was not for me, thank you very much.

In the meantime, the medical course of treatment for my heart defect continued to include the admonition, "just don't *do* anything." Doctors decided that gym at the junior high level would be too taxing. I was devastated. I longed to wear the drab olive-green jumpsuit uniform that had a special knack of making anyone who donned it look like a corpse who had succumbed to some dreadful disease. I wanted that look more than anything. I despised Mondays and Fridays as I headed for school without the requisite uniform under my arm. Finally, just as expected, fellow classmates began to notice and once again, I was different.

"Hey, how come *you* don't have a uniform?" The question was inevitable. I was standing at a crossroads. How could I deal with the impending judgement and rejection of my peers? I went with my only option.

"You know your heart?"

"Yeah."

"It goes *thump-thump*, right?"

"Ahhh, yeah, I guess."

"Well *my* heart goes *thump-psssh, thump-psssh.*" And then for added effect, I stepped into the face of my interrogator and with a snap of my fingers I would happily report, "If I take gym, I could go like THAT." Instant death. Instant death for a kid in junior high was way cool. I went from sick dork to celebrity status with a single snap of the fingers.

But the school still needed a place to put me while all my friends were in gym. Authority figures decided that I could grow up to be a librarian. This would be the perfect career for a heart patient, so in preparation for what had to be my true calling, they assigned me the job of library monitor. Thrilled with the prospects of shushing the library's patrons, a.k.a. my friends, I threw up in class just moments before I was scheduled to begin my first tour of duty. This should have been a clue to the authority figures. Eventually, I was placed in study hall after it was discovered that not only could I not shush, I was usually the cause of all the library disturbances.

So, as I continued toward adulthood, I clung to the only goal I felt I could one day achieve: that I would one day in the distant future be the proud owner of a fireplace.

One Step at a Time

I have a dream. It always begins the same way. The room is crowded with happy, friendly people. The bright lights accentuate the mood of the room, electrified with excited anticipation of what lies ahead. I stand in the crowd, my own excitement building, dressed in a gown made of yards and yards of sparkling material. The gown's mid-calf length reveals shoes manufactured with a triple purpose in mind: they can tap when necessary, but also function as a silk ballet slipper, and with a simple turn of the ankle, they become sleek, pointy, patent leather pumps with two-inch heels that never cause the varicose veins or cottage cheese thighs a moment's discomfort.

I am here to dance.

Then it happens. The lights dim and music begins to fill the room. The crowd, as if on cue, moves out onto the dance floor. I move with it, but as I step onto the hardwood floor, the crowd, which has been moving to the beat of the music, stops and turns. All eyes are on my partner as he waits for me. He holds his hand out, and as I place mine in his the world comes to a halt. The crowd steps back to make room, and my partner and I dance the night away, totally engrossed in what we are doing, ignoring the *oohs* and *aahs* of onlookers as we spin and dip and kick.

The chance of this dream ever happening in real life is as likely as my getting a call from Andrea Bocelli, begging me to join him at the Met to sing harmony. My singing ability results in a petition being anonymously placed in my mailbox every November, signed by all the members of my church, requesting that I lip-synch the upcoming selection of Christmas carols just to keep the holiday feeling festive.

And I sing a whole lot better than I dance.

I realized this sad flaw of mine the first night I laid eyes on Bill. It was the day after I arrived at college, and Bill, the president of the sophomore class, was responsible for the weekend-long freshman orientation. One of the orientation highlights was a pajama dance in the school cafeteria. My eccentric aunt, having no kids of her own, stepped in to function as Mom Number II. It was she who insisted all the years of my growing up that you must always wear your underwear with the knowledge that a grisly accident awaits you on this very day. Blood and guts were one thing, but what you *did not* want to do was repulse your medical caregivers with faded or stretched undies. My biological mother was much more concerned that I keep my room picked up, so my aunt assumed responsibility for keeping my sister, cousins, and me well-stocked with all sorts of clean, crisp underwear.

As college approached, this same aunt announced that a good education would never be possible without the requisite selection of designer night attire. She assured me that *everyone* in college would be dressed to the nines each evening as we curled up in our rooms to study. So I decided – she's footin' the bill – why not? A variety of lovely gowns, some with matching robes and slippers, was purchased and packed to ensure my education would be a quality one. And sure enough, the second day on campus a pajama dance was held.

Maybe it was the fact that I was the only one in the room wearing p.j.s that didn't have all manner of stains, tears, and holes in fabric whose color had long faded from hundreds if not thousands of washings. Perhaps it was simply ordained, but Bill walked across the room, our eyes locked, and he asked me to dance. And the second miracle to occur that night was that he *could* dance. He was the first man who was able to steer me across a room with ease and grace. He didn't even seem to notice that my own feet were jabbering after his in short taps like a massaging geisha's fingers gone mad. It was truly the start of something beautiful.

As we continued to date, girls would constantly pull Bill aside and whisper, "Give you a six-pack if you'll teach my boyfriend how to dance . . . just *promise* you'll never tell him I told you to." The good thing was this provided Bill and me with many a night's free refreshment in later months. The bad thing was it seemed Bill's talent on the dance floor could not be transferred to the occasional guy who would agree to a lesson.

I made a mental note – I would not request a dance lesson myself until after we were married, on the off chance that if Bill truly understood my lack of talent in this arena it might color his attitude toward me and perhaps even influence his impression of me as a suitable life partner.

The wedding was beautiful. Bill and I seemed to glide across the floor since I had grown so comfortable in his arms, but as others asked me to dance, I once again hopped and stumbled, leaving many a partner with a sore toe or black-and-blue thigh. The adage "there is no better dance than to dance with a bride" did not hold true as more and more people limped off after our spin around the floor.

But a clue was revealed when Bill and Pam, my new father and mother-in-law, stepped onto the floor, and proceeded to glide and swirl with the skill and grace of two champs. Dance was woven into Bill's genes from both his parents, and I would need to step up to the plate in order to hold my own in this family.

"Bill, teach me to dance," I later begged, and occasionally we would move around the kitchen floor. But Bill was not a trained dancer and instruction was slow and frustrating. So I finally decided, money talks. I would sign us *both* up for dance lessons, lest after solo lessons I would move to such a great skill level that Bill wouldn't be able to keep up. After much pleading I got Bill to agree to meet me at the Happy Feet Dance Academy after work.

The instructor had much to offer. She moved across the floor with every muscle in her body in perfect synch as Bill and I watched what was in store for us should we sign on as students. Then she escorted us to a small cubicle in the corner to discuss our options: we could take the basic course in which several simple moves would be taught, or we could opt for a premium package that included more-intense instruction plus an opportunity to return and dance along with other students on weekend nights. Or, if we were *really* serious, we could choose from their top of the line programs that extended years into our future and could potentially fill our every waking hour with dance. The choice was ours – it really depended on what we wanted to learn and just how good we wanted to be. I was sold. I wanted to be *good!* I had a *dream!*

But Bill, known to hold much tighter to a dollar bill than I, was not convinced. He hemmed and hawed about the cost of all these options until finally in my frustration I opened my purse and showed him that money was not going to be a problem. I had money to burn, and to prove it I proceeded to dump a wad of bills on the desk directly in front of our shocked but impressed potential Instructor Girl. At least *I* understood you excel in this life only if you are willing to invest in yourself.

Finally a compromise was reached. Bill and I would take the mid-level program, which would at least whet our appetite for future commitments. I was going to be a dancer at last.

Bill and I dutifully arrived for our first lesson just after work. Our own Personal Instructor Girl directed us to the floor and showed us some basic back-and-forth moves. This was going to be easy. All I had been lacking all these years was some instruction. After allowing us an initial attempt to repeat her steps, she added a swivel of her hips, ever so slight in its scope yet adding volumes to the overall effect of the dance. Bill dipped and swayed, producing an identical movement. It looked highly suspicious that he had lied to me about past lessons. I, on the other hand, was a little slower on the uptake. The step was hard enough, to add wiggle to that step was way beyond my capability.

Miss Personal Instructor Girl seemed patient and understanding at first, but as weeks progressed and I still was unable to add wiggle to my step, let alone execute an entire routine from memory, her willingness to exclaim that I was *close, oh, so close* seemed to wane. Finally, one afternoon it happened: Miss Hoity-Toity Personal Instructor Girl, pleased that Bill was not only keeping up but was showing signs of becoming a star pupil, casually asked if I would mind taking a seat in the row of chairs that lined the edge of the dance floor while she demonstrated a particularly difficult maneuver (one I had no hope of grasping) with Bill. I smiled. *Why, sure. Me mind? What would make you think that, Little Miss Hoity-Toity Personal Instructor Girl who is now cradled in my husband's arms? Why, who cares if it was I who emptied my entire life's savings on your desk just a few weeks ago and who cares if it was I who wanted to dance in the first place? No, Little Miss Hoity-Toity, Know-It-All Personal Instructor Girl, of COURSE I don't mind.*

I took my seat like a good girl and before I knew it the lesson for that day was over. And so it went: each day Bill and I would show up for our lesson and Little Miss Hoity-Toity, Know-It-All, Pain in the Tookus Personal Instructor Girl would suggest that I could really benefit by looking steadily at the two sets of feet that gently glided past me while I was firmly planted in the chair of my choice. Finally, the series of lessons I had paid for with my hard-earned savings was over, and as if on cue Little Miss Hoity-Toity, Know-It-All, Pain in the Tookus, Money Grubbing Personal Instructor Girl directed us back to her cubicle to once again review our lesson options in order to continue with *our* progress.

"So how'd you like to move on to a more advanced level of lessons?" she started.

"Lessons? *More lessons?* Over my dead body."

It took me about six months to lick my wounds and try again. Disco dancing. Yes, disco dancing lessons were being offered as a community education program, so I decided this was a better option. Unfortunately, I quickly found that disco utilizes even more wiggling and stepping than ballroom dancing. Bill, although ticked at first that he was being subjected to another pet project, once again took to the moves on the first attempt. As for me, I finally decided that it wasn't prudent to invest all that effort in a dance style that would probably be obsolete in several years, way before I had mastered any move.

My next plan required me to leave Bill at home. He absolutely *refused* to sign up for belly dancing lessons, although I'm sure he would have excelled had he given it half a chance. For me? It was a very sad thing, very sad indeed. Dancing would have to be relegated to my dreams.

Today I still dream, albeit a somewhat revised dream: I dream of the day when I dance. Except in this dream, the locale has changed. Now I dance in heaven; I dance in heaven with the dead Rockettes.

Morphing from "Doris" to "Scar Chest"

Think profound, life-saving medical advice comes only at the expense of thousands of dollars paid to some world-renowned specialist who labored for years in study and research? Think again. I learned of the medical course required to treat my birth defect via much more cost-efficient means. And this was not some minor ingrown toenail-type defect, this was a *heart* defect, a flaw that had killed many before me.

My whole medical condition was laid out one January afternoon as I curled up to read my latest issue of *Good Housekeeping* magazine. Prior to this, I had not been a big fan of *Good Housekeeping* magazine. I had ordered it purely out of obligation. For me, it was an instruction manual of sorts. It would dictate how I was supposed to live my life – what laundry detergent would make my colors their brightest, which flowering bulbs should usher in springtime grandeur.

Upon entering college years earlier, my roommate Crazy Marilyn and I had not been interested in bulbs or grandeur of any kind; rather, we were intrigued by the likes of Janis Joplin. So we decided to adopt the traits of a bad girl.

Smoke. Yes, that's it – we would smoke. Crazy and I pooled our money and blew fifty cents on a pack of Tareyton cigarettes, but not wanting the smell of smoke to infiltrate our freshly washed hair, we locked the door to our dorm room and donned shower caps as we lit up and puffed and coughed away. Somehow, the look of flowered shower caps wasn't in keeping with the Janis image, so we decided to take another route.

A joint. Yes, that's it – we'd smoke a joint. Then at least we wouldn't care if our hair smelled of smoke. So Crazy and I headed out to the far end of campus where we knew we'd find kids with joints. One puff or sip or whatever and I was out. Sound asleep. And I woke up to find that Crazy had had the time of her life, but I had missed the whole party and was now fully refreshed and ready to take over the cleanup duties. Joints looked as doubtful as the smokes, at least for me.

At the same time, a particularly friendly janitor on campus came up to me with a revelation. "You remind me of someone," he stated.

"I do? You wouldn't be thinking of *Janis* would you?"

"No, don't know her. Nope, this is someone *famous*, someone really special."

Well, special was good enough for the moment, and my new best friend promised to tell me which diva I reminded him of as soon as he could recall the name.

As the months continued and Crazy took to the library stacks dressed in a gorilla costume while I spent my time in the stacks with the works of Goethe, it became increasingly clear that my talent as a bad girl was limited at best. Then at the end of freshman year it all came together. Crazy Marilyn flunked out with such panache that the college review board would not even grant her a hearing, and I got my life sentence from my campus janitor friend.

"I *got* it! I know who you remind me of."

"Really, who?"

"Doris Day."

"Doris . . . *Day* . . . you mean the lady who makes her own ketchup and giggles like a hallway bubbler?"

"Yup, that's the one – Doris Day," he declared proudly.

Doris *Daay* . . . I was doomed. As his words sank in, I visualized myself barricaded behind a white picket fence in some small town in Iowa, carpooling my brood of kids in a wood-panel station wagon, serving Kool Aid from a smiley-face pitcher while wearing snowy white Carter's Spanky Pants, whose unsightly panty lines would ban me from ever stepping foot in my local Victoria's Secret. Didn't my janitor friend realize that beneath all my bubbly lay a frustrated bad girl? No. That side of me would never be allowed to come out. Instead I would marry Bill, my college sweetheart, and promptly upon saying "I do," I would order a subscription of *Good Housekeeping* magazine.

Yes, it was true. I was a die-hard Doris Day. Doris to my very core.

January 1978, several years after coming to grips with the Doris thing, my life was forever changed by *Good Housekeeping*. As a new bride who months earlier had moved with Bill to Chicago, I noticed an article titled "Twin Girls Have Identical Surgery." The article described two identical twin sisters who were born with identical holes in their hearts. What? *I* have a hole in *my* heart! Between the top two chambers, this hole in the twins' hearts was called atrial septal defect. No *kidding*. *I* have an atrial septal defect. Symptoms included irregular heartbeats and fatigue. Get outta town . . . *I* have bad heartbeats and get tired easily. The article continued by describing how doctors were able to patch the holes during open-heart surgery.

Open-heart surgery? Nope. Thanks anyway – not for me. Ain't gonna go there. Up to this point, open-heart surgery was for famous people like John Wayne and Jackie Gleason, not for Doris. It made headline news. It made red, ugly scars. It made people die. No. Thank you very much, open-heart surgery was not for me.

That was the day I entered my denial stage. As my heartbeats became increasingly weird, I developed similarly weird remedies to offset them. I decided that rapid beats must have meant I was nervous, so I incorporated calming techniques, like stroking. I found a smooth oval rock, which fit securely in the palm of my hand, and whenever my beats would increase or skip, I would close my eyes, hum softly and gently rub the surface of my rock. An external pacemaker of sorts. As I was becoming increasingly dependent on my stroking therapy, I couldn't help notice the odd looks I was getting as I hummed and stroked and hummed. I decided to hum in my head.

Then I concluded that my irregular heartbeats were all my boss's fault. He was a flaming idiot. I needed to eliminate him from my life. This obese man, who repeatedly described the debilitating thyroid condition from which he suffered, would lock himself in his office for hours on end. Then my department cohorts and I would take turns knocking on his door under some pretext so we could see what flavor donut he was eating at the time. Sometimes his face was covered in powdered sugar, other times a dab of strawberry jelly hung from his chin. While this provided a great source of entertainment, I needed to move on for my health. I applied for a position in another department and was happy to make the move. Interestingly, though, my bad heartbeats made the move with me.

Things were starting to get serious psychologically and physically. Open-heart surgery, if one were to survive, meant a big ugly red scar from neck to waist. At the ripe old age of 25, I would never again be able to wear anything other than turtlenecks. I took to studying people's necklines, and found few outfits that would hide my disfigurement. My husband would leave me for a sexy number in string bikini. I would be forced to join a convent, if only to reap the benefit of their flowing garb. The Sisters would assign me the task of tinkling a little bell as I begged for alms while sitting on a stool next to the hot dog vendor inside the lobby of some discount department store. I was becoming a mental invalid courtesy of my vivid imagination.

And physically, things were taking a turn for the worse, too. Bright lights and the perky jingles of TV commercials were enough to put me into an arrhythmia. Trips upstairs needed to be rationed with exceptional adeptness so my husband wouldn't notice my plight. I prayed there wouldn't be a fire in the neighborhood because the excitement of seeing a fire truck whiz by would surely kill me. I decided I needed to see a doctor. I was becoming desperate.

I got out the Yellow Pages, found a doctor and made an appointment.

"So what brings you here today?" the doctor asked as he scanned my newly created chart.

"I need open-heart surgery, sir."

"Say what?"

"I need open-heart surgery."

"Really now . . . and what makes you think that?"

"*Good Housekeeping* told me, sir – the January issue."

"You're here because *Good Housekeeping* told you to have open-heart surgery?"

"Yes. Actually, I thought my rock would help, but that doesn't seem to be working anymore."

"A *rock* told you, too?" The doctor paused to jot some notes down in my chart.

"No, sir, that's silly. The rock is for stroking and humming. That seemed to work for a while but now I'm having problems with commercials. I am having a hard time breathing during the commercials. And noise and bright lights – I'm not good with them, either."

"Ahhh, I see." The doctor smiled. "You're a new patient here, aren't you? Where are you from?"

I somehow thought he suspected I was visiting from some strange planet. He obviously wasn't up on his *Good Housekeeping,* and I bet he didn't watch a whole lot of TV either.

"I'm from New Jersey."

"Ahhh, *now* I see." Somehow, New Jersey seemed to be a clue. He stroked his chin as he pondered all the wisdom of his medical training and experience while he continued to make notes in my chart.

"Honey, let me offer you some advice. You've just moved away from home. You're obviously homesick and you miss your mother . . . I would go home and have a baby, if I were you."

"A baby?"

"Yes, it would do you good, give you something to occupy your time. Keep you focused. Go home and have a baby."

"That's it?"

"Well no, there will be a charge for the office visit. You can see the receptionist."

And with that, I was sent on my way. I headed home with great joy. This was a first for me – a doctor's visit where I didn't need to get undressed, a cardiac visit that didn't even include a stethoscope. At least there was nothing wrong with me. I was fine. Bill and I ordered pizza to celebrate the good news.

But the crazy beats kept coming and soon Bill began to notice how I would hobble over to the couch to veg out every moment I could.

"I've made you an appointment with a specialist, a cardiologist," he finally announced. This doctor promised to be a touch more knowledgeable than the last one, and he actually made me get undressed, which was a good sign. The first thing he did was dab little blobs of jelly all over me in order to attach the electrodes of an EKG machine. With his back to me, he began to push buttons, causing a strip of paper to funnel through what looked like a lie-detector machine. Totally engrossed in his work, he suddenly started to grumble as he hit the side of the machine with his fist.

"Bear with me here for a minute. Something's not right." As he continued to hover over the tape that was diagramming my heartbeat, it seemed that the lie detector was very unhappy with impulses my heart was sending. Instead of recording a steady rhythmic pulse, the needle would fly off the top of the paper every few beats. After a second bang of his fist, the doctor stooped to pull the plug from the electric outlet, hoping this would bring his machine back to its senses. Alas, as the recording continued to baffle the doctor, he eventually gave up and pulled off the stickies that adorned my naked chest.

Next, he placed a stethoscope to my chest, and was clearly intrigued by the sounds he heard. Then as he leaned in to listen more closely, I stared up into his jet-black mop of hair, a thick black mass caked with dandruff. Elvis, the King, with dandruff. As I peered upward from the gurney, I realized that any movement on my part, however slight, could possibly cause one of those flakes to drop down onto my face, perhaps even into my nostrils. I squeezed my eyes tight in a desperate effort to remain motionless. I wanted to die.

"So how'd it go?" Bill asked anxiously as he waited for my return.

"Not good." I blurted, "I'm not going back."

"Not going back? Why not? What does the doctor think?"

"I think he thinks I'm sick but that's his problem. I'm not going back. He's got dandruff."

"DANDRUFF? You can't reject a doctor just because he's got a little *dandruff*," Bill countered. "And besides, he's supposed to be smart. He's a specialist, for God's sake."

"First, this is not *just a little dandruff*. This is great big chunks of white gunk. At any moment one of them could fall and hit me in the head, possibly knock me out or if it landed in my nostril I would suffocate for sure. Besides, how *smart* can a doctor be if he doesn't realize he is one disgusting human being? I'm NOT going back."

I'd had enough. Obedient Doris was morphing into a strong, opinionated woman. I now had criteria – any medical specialist from here on out would have to be smart *and* cute. Things were getting serious. A campaign was launched. I was on a mission. I would spare no effort and no expense to find the smartest, cutest doctor on the face of the earth; if he was familiar with cardiology, so much the better. Female doctors would not be exempt from my quest; however, they would have to hold up to the same standards and unwavering scrutiny as male doctors, and it was doubtful I could ever develop the hots for a woman doctor as I was hoping to do with my male selection. If I was going to be sliced and diced and forced to participate in any number of humiliating, painful remedies, dang it, I was going to do it in style.

I asked everyone I came in contact with, "Do you have a doctor?" Yes. "Does he have unsightly nose hairs? Bad breath? Unusual twitches or facial ticks? Large, protruding ears? Festering acne? Underarm stains or stink? Boils? Warts? Does he drool when he speaks? Does he have *dandruff*?" 'No' to all of the above resulted in an option I was willing to consider.

Interestingly, all fingers began to point to an internist who had treated a woman in my department during her bypass surgery. The good news was she was still alive and she loved her doctor. I made an appointment.

My new doctor was cute in a grandfatherly way and his style was slow and purposeful, a style that balanced my hyper-emotional one. Once again I was hooked up to an EKG machine and once again the needle recording my heart beat flew off the paper, since the machine manufacturer had never anticipated a whacko beat like the one I was producing. Instead of banging on the side of the monitor and unplugging and replugging it, my new doctor just said "hmmm." I liked his style. Then he sent me for a chest X-ray, which came back showing an enlarged heart. He said this was an indicator that my heart was working extra hard – *no duh*. It was like my heart was pumpin' iron during all those commercials. It was one tough heart muscle that had caused that EKG needle to go flying.

"So how are you feeling?"

"Me? . . . Oh, never better . . . just doing swell, really," I lied. *WHAT? What is the MATTER with you?* a voice screamed deep inside my head. *NEVER BETTER? You are on death's door, for cripes sake! TELL HIM THE TRUTH.*

"Well, I'd like to follow you more closely, so why don't you make an appointment for, let's say, three months from now. Would that be okay?"

"Sure, that'd be fine," I smiled. *FINE? F I N E? You'll be DEAD – D-E-A-D – in three months. DO YOU HEAR ME?* the inner voice raged.

"Thanks. It was a pleasure meeting you," my audible voice continued.

A significant battle was waging in my head. The smart side of my brain knew I was in big trouble and sinking fast. The emotional side of my brain was scared to death and yet it still clung to the hope that some home remedy could be found in lieu of that big, red, ugly scar.

Then a conversation with my sister Chris changed everything. We were to spend the day frolicking together at the beach.

"So, how's it going?" she asked. "Rudy? . . . Rudy?"

My face screwed up. My chin started to quiver and I squeezed my lips tight to try and keep sounds from coming out. Why'd she have to go and do a dumb thing like that? Why did she have to ask me how things were going? As we sat on a blanket with happy children playing all around us, the floodgates opened. It started as a low moan and quickly accelerated into a deep guttural howling, the howling of a wounded animal that moved into convulsing sobs, soaking the towel we had so carefully laid out of reach of the water's edge.

"Hey, Mommy, look!" Chris's son found it hard to believe an adult could produce the flood of tears that 3-year-olds in a bad mood are famous for. "Aunt Rudy's *crying.*"

I attempted to tame the sobs and reply, "Me? Never better," but somehow I didn't think she would buy that response. There was no more faking it, no more rocks, no more lies. I needed help, and breaking down in front of my sister, who also happened to be an RN, and not just an ordinary RN but a cardiac intensive care RN, meant there was no turning back.

"You're going to go back to your doctor and tell the truth – or *I* will."

Shit.

I called my new doctor and told him we needed to chat. His office was in the Chicago Loop, which meant I had to take the subway from my office. As I stepped off the train, I looked up at the flight of stairs that led up to the sidewalk. I might as well have been told to climb Mount Everest. A street lady who was dragging all her worldly possessions in a shopping bag stepped on the bottom step along side of me. Street people are not really known for their perky attitude and zippy step but this woman had vim and vigor I could only dream of. With each step as she moved ahead of me the voice in my head screamed out, H*ey, wait . . . lady, wait for me!* When I finally reached the sidewalk, my baglady friend was long gone and I was so winded I had to lean against the Marshall Field's department store window, gasping for breath. People passing by pointed and stared, conjuring up all sorts of reasons why this business woman was plastered against the window.

"I'm not doing too well," was all I needed to say when I finally arrived for my appointment.

"We'll get you in the next available bed," my doctor said, not the least bit surprised. He might as well have ordered me to turn myself in to the local prison. I had walked through hospital corridors, always holding my breath to keep the hospital stink out of my nostrils. They were full of people – sad, pathetic, germy, contagious people. They were all prisoners on death row and now I was going to be one of them. But, then, my doctor said something interesting.

"You know, I'm quite optimistic."

"Optimistic? You mean it? Like . . . things will be okay?"

"Yes, I'm very optimistic." This statement began a game, an unspoken ritual of sorts, and we would play it every day for the next three weeks as I was tested and sliced and diced. Each day as my doctor would visit, he would sit back in his chair, cross his gangly legs and say, "I'm optimistic." That would be my clue that I was still alive. I clung to that assessment like a drowning person clings to a plank of wood. Maybe this wasn't going to be so awful after all.

Then I walked into my assigned room. A woman who filled every inch of her bed also filled every inch of air space with her moans and groans, which were punctuated with sudden sharp, bloodcurdling squeals, ending in high-pitched screams. She would have made a great sound track person for a Hollywood sci-fi thriller. The nurse didn't seem to notice. The lady had digestion problems. I diagnosed it as acute intestinal failure with death impending. The hospital people saw it another way and cheerfully announced that she was well enough to go home the next day. Home? This is what you guys call *healthy*? I wanted to disagree until it dawned on me that her going home meant I would get a new roommate. I decided to take my chances as anything was better than trying to make it through another night with this screamer.

Things were looking up as the new day dawned. Papers were being signed to ship my roomie and her screams home. I relaxed in a bed that provided endless entertainment with all the positions you can create with just the click of a button. My TV played soaps I had not watched since my college days. Food that I had personally selected off a menu the previous day arrived on dishes that would not even require washing on my part. This was going to be OK, really.

Then The Nurse arrived. As she stood in the doorway, she bellowed with The Question of the Day: "So, Mrs. Wilson, have we had our bowel movement today?"

"Beg your pardon?" *What do you mean 'we'? We have done nothing of the sort and we do not anticipate doing it in the near future either, not that it's any of your business anyway.*

"Shhh . . ." I plucked the sheet off my knees, which were at this moment elevated to a High-Knee,

High-Back mattress position, and from behind this fabric screen, I pointed and nodded over to my roommate. "*She's* the one with the digestive problems. I'm only here with a bum heart."

"Now, Mrs. Wilson. We note this on *all* our patients. So, tell me, *have* we had our bowel movement today?" I was sure I had seen this lady before. Perhaps she had starred in some movie depicting Nazi occupation during World War II. Her eyes seemed to cut right through to my very core; her smile was just a little too smiley, and her finger was itching to record the exact gory details of my latest BM on her clip chart. Perhaps she had done a stint on German Romper Room before becoming a nurse.

"No, *we* have not."

If these people were going to get hung up on stuff like this, I was going to be in big trouble. You see, I have a bit of a hang-up. I can't . . . I *don't* . . . go to the bathroom unless I have uninterrupted quiet time surrounded by my own personally selected Waverly wallpaper.

It's never been a very big deal, except of course that year I went off to college, until it dawned on me that my entire dorm went to dinner at the same time which allowed me the opportunity to make up some excuse to run back and at least enjoy peace and quiet in my own personally selected booth.

Then there was that summer spent in Europe. It was then that I cowered in my hotel room all night rather than use a hall bathroom. This was a good indication I would never grow up to be an international spy or have a career in roadside construction; you weren't going to get me into one of the curbside port-o-potties while all the world whizzed by, faces pressed hard against the windows to see who had to go pee pee.

Vacations were also a challenge until I trained my husband to take long, long walks whenever he was ordered. I thought I had grown quite mature in that I was at least willing to forego the Waverly on rare occasions.

Hospital bathrooms ranked right up there with festival outhouses as far as being a place of solitude and stylish décor. Never – it was never going to happen here.

A simple 'no' got the nurse off my back the first morning and I thought my problem was solved. Until day two and then day three. When I tried to explain my condition, Miss Nazi Romper Room bristled. She had the nerve to inform me that I was being ridiculous, that my hang-up was unhealthy. I begged to differ as, other than a bum heart, I was in overall pretty good shape and certainly a whole lot better than my first roommate. So by day four, I decided to try another tack. I lied. It worked.

"Mrs. Wilson, have we had our bowel movement today?"

"Ohhh, yes and it was a doozy. Thanks *ever so* for asking." And she was gone. Done deal. Chart noted. Why didn't I think of that earlier? Function like a politician: just tell 'em what they want to hear and everybody's happy.

Then a young guy pushing a wheelchair arrived. "Mrs. Wilson? I'm here to take you to your treadmill test."

"Treadmill test? My doctor never mentioned he wanted me to do a treadmill test."

"Well, they're waiting for you down in the lab, so come on board." My chauffeur cheerfully waved me on to the wheelchair.

"You know, this doesn't make sense. My doctor never mentioned I was going for a treadmill test," I chimed in as soon as I arrived at the lab. "Are you sure?"

"Yes, Mrs. Wilson," the technician stated as she began to adjust the leads that were attached to my chest.

"Are you *really* sure?"

"Mrs. Wilson . . . the order's right here . . . Ruby Wilson."

"Ruby? Did you say, *Roo Beee?*" Oops! Another heart patient was sitting somewhere, probably watching *my* soaps, wondering why they were running late on her treadmill test. I made a mental note:

NO COMA ALLOWED or at least not until my little friend Ruby kicked the bucket.

The thing my internist *did* tell me was that a surgeon would be stopping by to visit. Yeah, right, just pay me a visit – no strings attached. And this guy had not been subjected to my rigorous pre-screening. I was concerned.

Then – just as soap opera hunk Trent poured himself a cognac from the library decanter while explaining that Maybrey could not be carrying his child because a war injury had rendered him sterile – in walked my surgeon. No – not just a surgeon – a Greek god. A perfect melding of Robert Redford and Paul Newman with a sprinkling of Mel Gibson in the eyes, a flawless human specimen if I ever saw one. If I had had my own library decanter, I would have poured him a drink. I would have borne him a child, just like Maybrey was doing for someone, just as my first doctor had suggested. I was in love and my heartbeat, which couldn't handle a Sesame Street review of the alphabet, was going wild.

"Hi. My name is Doctor Monson."

Take me away. I'm all yours. We were meant to be together.

"Hi, it's nice to meet you." Did I detect a spark when we shook hands? Does he feel it, too? Hospital life was sure looking up and *thank God* I was in for a bum heart and not some disgusting intestinal problem. I got to bare my chest to the man of my dreams (it doesn't get better than that) until of course the test results come back and they indicate surgery is called for, but in the meantime I was happy, yes, very happy indeed.

Unfortunately, my surgeon was not the only person I got to bare my chest for. When Chris realized I needed to be in a hospital, she warned me about the unfortunate timing of my bum heart beats.

"You need to be in a teaching hospital because that's where cutting-edge technology is done. But there is a down side – you are going to be in a teaching hospital in the month of July." This translates to: you are going to be in a hospital full of medical students whose degrees in doctoring aren't old enough for the ink to have dried, but have now been turned loose on poor unsuspecting patients and they *think* they know *everything*.

"This is even further complicated in your case, because you're young, you don't have a disgusting condition, you are fairly conversant and somewhat cute, so each and every month-old doctor will make it a personal mission to cure you," she continued.

Well, with a newbie assigned to do my intake evaluation, or in other words ask and record every possible question about my past life and health (except for my preference in bathroom wallpaper), it didn't take long for word to get out that a live one was in bed 416B. Doctors who looked like children came at all hours of the day and night "to take a listen," and since my heartbeat was wild enough to stump the machines, the med students and newbie docs were thrilled with the sounds I was producing. This kept them coming back for more.

Doctors would tiptoe in my room in the middle of the night and whisper, "Do you mind. . ." This was my signal to bare my chest and just hang out as they were being entertained or educated or probably a little of both. It was also my excuse to socialize.

"You know, I'm sure I'm headed for surgery."

"Surgery? Oh, no. You don't want that," one resident whispered while on his midnight visit. "I've heard it's sooo painful, you can't even breathe . . . they have to teach you how to breathe in a whole new way so you don't move your chest!"

Breathe a whole new way? Pain? PAIN? This had never even been mentioned before. What was I doing? Was I out of my mind? Was my hunk of a surgeon really worth it? Those bad beats weren't all that bad and besides, if I moved to a ranch, or better yet, moved to a comfy chair in a comfy ranch, most of my problems would be solved. I shook with terror, thanks to my vocal, yet stupid, midnight visitor.

"Dr. Phelan, you never mentioned the pain. You owe it to me to tell me the truth about the pain," I began my next morning visit with my internist.

"What are you talking about?"

"The pain after surgery. You know, the pain that hurts so much you can't breathe."

"Who have you been talking to?"

"Oh, that doctor with the red hair and freckles. He came by last night to take a listen." My very docile doctor seemed to tense, if only for a second.

"I'll be right back," he said as he unwrapped his gangly legs and headed out the door. Sometime later, he returned, refolded his legs into our standard conversation mode and continued, "I think you have been misinformed. While there is always some pain with any surgery, we have meds that can take care of that so you don't have to worry. As far as teaching you how to breathe? That's a new one. I've never heard that one before. I'm actually quite optimistic."

"Optimistic?" I breathed a sigh of relief courtesy of the old style of breathing. We were back on track. "*Really? Really* optimistic?" I somehow needed to hear it again.

"Yes, frankly I'm very optimistic."

"What happened in *here* today?" my afternoon nurse asked as soon as she arrived for her shift. "The docs are still shaking and I understand they have been totally *banished* from ever entering your room again!"

I realized at that moment there was a redheaded, freckled-faced doctor who was just a tad smarter than he had been the night before and who probably also wished he wasn't quite so distinctive looking. Lesson learned: keep your mouth shut when you don't have a clue. And this was all thanks to my doctor, whose power within the hospital was beginning to show. And power somehow always makes a man look cuter.

Each day we moved a step closer to the inevitable, and finally, when all the reports were in, the consensus was: surgery. I wondered why these experts hadn't just taken *Good Housekeeping* a little more seriously. A lot of expense and effort could have been avoided, but then again, I'm just a lowly subscriber with a bad beat, what do I know?

The bearer of the good news/bad news was Doctor Adonis himself. Good news: I would once again be able to revel in happy perky commercials without going into cardiac arrest (you always love the things you can't have). Bad news: they were going to do some serious slicing, dicing and hacksawing, leaving behind a big, ugly, red scar in order to enable me to watch those same happy perky commercials. Since I was falling deeper and deeper in love with Adonis-doc, I decided that breaking down into a sobbing, convulsing, goo-oozing-out-of-my-nostrils blob would not do much to advance our relationship, so I just smiled and said, "Okay. Let's go for it."

The plan was to patch the hole in my heart, and a pig valve would be waiting in case my mitral valve needed to be replaced. Now the concept of having a pig part in one's body could lend itself to some really cool fun except for the fact that pigs are very old and frail by the age of 10. So, if I would be the beneficiary of a pig part, I'd need to come back for a re-do within 10 years, not something I relished doing ... except ... that would mean I could rekindle my relationship with Adonis-doc and we would both be more mature and ready to take that next step and ...

I was scheduled to be patient number four out of a possible four the following Monday. Since this was pre-cost-containment days, the plan was for me to put a few more days in my Barcalounger bed over the weekend in order to be prepped. Prepping meant that I would take a field trip to the intensive care unit to see where I would wake up after surgery, a thoughtful gesture that only instilled total internal hysteria as I looked around at the current ICU occupants and realized what a mess they all were (which justified their being in ICU in the first place). The remainder of my time was spent watching TV, drinking what seemed like gallons of potassium, which in its liquid form tastes like urine with a slightly salty aftertaste (if I could make my best guess what urine must taste like), showering, watching TV, showering, and then showering again.

I wondered if, when all this was over, I shouldn't call up the folks at Dial soap and suggest we make a commercial, a particularly happy perky one, where I could expound on the virtues of their product: if a drop-dead gorgeous surgeon recommends Dial soap to get patients squeaky clean prior to open-heart surgery, just think what it can do for you on your next big date? Adonis-doc and I could run slow-motion through a field of wild flowers, coddling a bar of Dial soap. Then, while embraced in each other's arms . . . poor Bill. I told him that when all this was over, if I didn't show up for dinner one night, he should check Adonis-doc's front stoop before turning in a missing person's report. Bill said, "Okay." He wasn't the least bit ruffled by my infatuation. Anything was better than Dumb-doc and Dandruff-doc.

Then, The Big Day arrived. Bill showed up promptly at 6 a.m. with his daily fix of Oscar Mayer bologna slapped between two slices of Wonderbread – the extent of his culinary creativity and expertise. I was starting to shrivel around the edges in my newfound cleanliness. Nurses kept checking in on me – possibly to verify that I had not made a bee-line for the back stairs in a last-ditch effort to escape the knife. What they didn't realize was I was physically not capable of making a run for anything, much less stairs.

We had been cautioned early on that if there were any complications with earlier patients, I would be the one bumped. Sure enough, number three had the nerve to go and do something complicated and rude, like not to breathe when the heart-lung machine was turned off. So at mid-morning, I got the word that we were a no go. Instead I was told "just keep showering." Bill went out and bought a new slab of Oscar Mayer.

My new slot: number one on Wednesday, which had thoughtfully been made available by some little kid with a bum heart who now also had the chicken pox. This was good news. The rumor out on the street is that Wednesday is the day to have surgery. It was suggested that the OR staff is too blaah on Mondays after their wild and crazy weekend and on Fridays they were too focused on the upcoming wild and crazy weekend. Apparently, dull and studious folks never make it in the surgical profession. But on Wednesday, everybody would be fresh and ready to do some serious surgerying. Also, being number one had its advantage: again, staff happy and perky like the commercials.

This meant two more days of wash and watch, wash and watch. Maybrey was still trying to figure out who fathered her child, but I wasn't concerned. Soap Opera Rule #1: Nothing of any consequence shall ever occur on Tuesday, Wednesday or Thursday. I figured Maybrey wouldn't have her problem solved before I was released from ICU. For that matter, she'd probably still be in a quandary over her 10-year-old kid if I needed to return to my Barcalounger bed for a new piggy part.

Wednesday AM would not have been complete without a mini-crisis, which occurred when a very sick patient had the nerve to show up in the middle of the night needing emergency open-heart surgery. He was assigned my time slot, bumping me back into wash-and-watch mode. Then my surgeon showed up for work (did I mention the fact that he was drop dead gorgeous?). Once again, power won out. My surgeon threw a fit, so the sick guy was handed a remote control, filled in briefly on Maybrey's plight, and told to wait his turn, like everybody else. I was back on within half an hour – just enough time for one last quick once-over with the Dial soap, in case a few invisible buggies had invaded my body during the crisis.

As the gurney arrived, Bill and I said our good-byes – not easy despite my doctor's optimistic outlook. TV makes good-byes look so loving, so passionate, but in real life the clock is ticking and words better be short and sweet 'cause there is a business to run. Before I knew it, I was plopping my prune butt onto the operating table with a mass of people like a swarm of ants converging from all directions. With eyes peering through scrubs, nurses and technicians advised me of every pinch and prick, suggesting fire ants. Finally, it was time to count backwards from 100 to 0. I didn't even make it to 97.

The next thing I knew, courtesy of my previous field trip, I was in ICU Bed Number 3. *Bed* is a real misnomer. Easy access is key in ICU, so patients lie stark naked on gurneys lined side by side with curtains that are closed only on rare occasions. Nurses scurried about attending to my every need, most of which I had no clue I even needed.

Bill was right there, too, rubbing my forehead with the tip of his finger as this was the only part of me that was not medically engaged. I was a mess, with five IVs and tubes coming from every hole in my body, in addition to holes which hadn't been there hours earlier. Pretty is not a priority in the ICU.

In addition, there was a big pipe sticking out of my throat, which was breathing for me. The respirator. With limited options on how to occupy my time, I plotted my revenge. Revenge against the designers, manufacturers, packagers, shippers, and any medical person who played a role in my having a respirator pressing on the back of my throat. For one split second, I visualized Adonis-doc with a respirator crammed down *his* throat and a tiny tear spilling from his Mel Gibson eyes. The designers must have forgotten that the tongue is also attached to the back of the throat, rendering it an inconvenient obstruction. I decided breathing wasn't all that important so I tried to spit the pipe out. Not a good plan as the thing must have been anchored deep in my lungs. My nurse leaned over and whispered, "Why don't you go back to sleep. That thing will be gone in no time." Good idea and sleep was certainly not a problem.

Twenty-four hours passed. A 24-hour nap that also happened to be my 26th birthday. I vaguely remember a cluster of people standing around my gurney holding up a cake and singing "Happy Birthday" prior to their heading off to the break room to inhale it in honor of my big day. They told me it was delicious. Bill, the ultimate romantic, presented me with a gift-wrapped 32-cup percolator. Even in my drug-induced stupor, I wondered, "What was he *thinking*??" Then the nursing staff took my percolator off to the break room as coffee added a nice little touch to my party. My body was still plugged into the wall behind my gurney, or I'm sure someone would have thought of inviting me to join in the festivities.

As I continued to improve, I was moved from intensive-Intensive Care to not-so-intensive-Intensive Care, which meant I would get a real bed again and a private room.

"Okay, Mrs. Wilson. We're going to go for a walk," my nurse announced.

"*Walk?* Are you *crazy?* Did you check your notes? Do you have any clue why I'm in here? I just had open-heart surgery, for God's sake!"

"Yes, Mrs. Wilson, I know. I was your nurse when you came down from the OR."

"Oh . . . then . . . what do I need to say to convince you I *can't* walk. How 'bout *you* walk and I'll watch."

"Nice try."

And that was how my days were spent. I begged. I pleaded. I attempted to shame the nurses, bribe them, *anything* in order to cajole them into giving me a reprieve. But they weren't the least bit fazed. I needed to walk. Some brilliant medical folks somewhere who obviously had never even been near a knife, no less one that slices open your chest in order for hacksaws and braces to bust open your chest to tinker with your heart, decided that walking was good for recovery.

And they were right.

Not that I like to admit when others are right, but everyday I showed exciting promise, if exciting means you walked the length of your bed unassisted. By the week's end, I was ready to go home.

This came as bittersweet news. I was no longer going to have my daily visits with Adonis-doc and all the nurses that I had grown so fond of (despite what they thought of that pain-in-the-butt patient in 1422A).

My parents, who had been put on hold as per Bill's and my wishes, made plans to fly out and care for both of us. When my mom heard of Bill's 21-day diet of Oscar Mayer and Wonderbread, she directed her mothering toward him, baking goodies as her way of celebrating my recovery and thanking him for his unending love and support.

After a week at home, I was bored and ready to venture out into the real world. A pick-your-own blueberry farm was a traditional summer outing, so my mom and I decided to get us some blueberries to open up all sorts of new baking options. As we arrived at the farm, we were assigned a bush. Our plan was for me to sit on the ground and pick the bottom half of the bush and my mother would stand over me and pick the top half. Just to make sure I didn't do anything stupid, she admonished me with, "And the *minute* you feel tired, you tell me and we're going home."

With that, an old geezer on the next bush looked over at us and hissed, "You know, THAT'S what's wrong with you young people today..." With eyes glistening, he stabbed his finger down in my direction so I would truly grasp the sad fact that *I* was the bane of civilization, the reason for everything that was wrong with the world.

"Sir," I smiled up sweetly. "You'll have to forgive me. I'm not quite myself. You see, I had open-heart surgery two weeks ago."

Wow! Was that ever cool. Single-handedly I put the nosey old coot into cardiac arrest. Nah, nah, nah, nah, nah!

My progress continued, and sadly, I was released from Adonis-doc's care. Six months after my surgery I had joined a health club and learned, for the first time, how to sweat. After showering one day, I stood at my locker wrapped in only a towel. A woman from across the locker room pointed and stared at my scar.

"Oh my God! *You've had open-heart surgery!*"

"Yes," I looked down at my scar. "I have."

And with that, the woman slumped and started to cry. Now I knew my scar was a tad on the gross side, but this reaction seemed a bit over the top. It turned out this lady had a 3-year-old son who had been born with a hole in his heart, just like I had. And his doctor, who turned out to be none other than Adonis-doc himself, wanted to operate. But the mother couldn't agree to it. She didn't want her son to hurt.

I sat down with her and held her hand. I told her that yes, it would hurt, but there are meds that can deal with that. And, if she allowed her son to go through with the surgery she would be giving him the gift of baseball and running and things I was never allowed to do. We held each other until the tears had all dried, and then I believe a mom went off to make a very important phone call to her son's drop-dead gorgeous doctor.

As I finished dressing, I looked down at my chest. Where a big, ugly, red scar had been, I now saw a souvenir, a gift that I could pass on to a young boy and his mom in the form of baseball and sports and . . .

Diagnosis: Black Lab Nut

As an expert on being sick, I am keenly aware of disease. Some diseases are clearly visible and debilitating, while others are not so obvious to the naked eye but are nonetheless chronic, all-encompassing, and financially burdensome. I first learned of this particular condition when I read of a fellow sufferer in the newspaper. An article described a man who, on his way home from work, stopped to save a puppy that was stranded in a raging river. When the reporter asked the man what possessed him to risk his life for a puppy, the man shrugged and said, "I don't know. I own a black Lab, and I guess I just love animals."

On the surface, you might say, "Ah, animal lover," but that is too bland, too weak a description of this man's condition. This condition is extreme, like a double espresso is to Rhode Island coffeemilk. His seemingly innocent remark, understood in its entirety, speaks volumes about a rarely documented affliction – a Black Lab Nut.

The most significant difference between an animal lover and a Black Lab Nut is that the former sees animals as just that – animals. Dogs are "best friends." The Black Lab Nut, on the other hand, sees animals as extensions of themselves – as children who happen to walk on four legs instead of two – a mere anatomical difference. Children who, despite a very long and active puppyhood, are ever defended by their loving parents, like the glassy-eyed mothers and fathers who stare into the TV camera on the nightly news mumbling, "Not my Jimmy. He ain't done nuthin'. My Jimmy, he's a goood boy," even though the crime scene was dripping with Jimmy's DNA.

Typically, other children – such as two-legged humans, rodents, reptiles, and most especially, cats – are also present in the homes of Black Lab Nuts. Some kind of keen instinct seems to be bred into cats that are hunting for an adoptive family. When they smell the perfume of black Lab, they know they are dealing with two-legged suckers, and they move in.

When evaluating and selecting a home, the local school district means nothing to a Black Lab Nut. However, issues such as whether there's a safe place for Mergatroid to play, or if Duke can see out the windows, are determining factors in selecting a residence.

Holidays for Black Lab Nuts are celebrated in a way that reflects this parent/child relationship. Gifts are selected with care, wrapped and presented to the four-legged children while the two-legged ones patiently sit and wait their turn. Birthday cakes topped with marshmallows sculpted and frosted to look like fire hydrants are served up to guests, often other neighborhood four-legged friends who have received an invitation to come by for cake, cookies, games, and a gift exchange. Party hats and blowers are customary but usually more for the pleasure of the two-legged guests.

As with many diseases, this condition may lie dormant for years only to rear its ugly head as circumstances evolve. If two people who carry the gene happen to marry, life can get interesting. Really interesting.

I always knew I was an animal lover. Our family dog, a chubby little dachshund named Lumpi, taught me about love. When I was six, he ate the head off my Ginny doll, but despite the horror of it all I could not hate him. When I was eight, I was presented with my first Bible, a large cumbersome book with no pictures. I was skeptical, but I was told that this book was the key to life. It was going to get me into heaven.

One of the first things you did with a new book was pencil your name in just behind the front cover. This kept lost books to a minimum. As I wrote out my name, I thought, if this book was going to help me get into heaven, why not create some extra insurance for a problem I had pondered many times. So I penciled Lumpi's name next to mine. There. If God was going to judge dogs, as I was told He would one day judge me, how could He turn His back on a chubby little dachshund whose name was clearly printed in the front cover of a Bible? I was pleased with my foresight.

Then, one week later, just as I returned home from church with my family, I heard my name called from the front room. My parents sat stiffly on the camelback couch. With its silk brocade, anyone sitting on this couch needed to sit straight up or they'd slide right off the edge, but for some reason on this particular morning my parents seemed stiffer than normal.

"What's this?" my father demanded as he held my Bible open to the front cover. "Well . . . that's my name," I whispered. I had a good idea where all this was going.

"Aaand?"

"Ah . . . Lumpi . . ." I knew perfectly well that my father could read the large bold letters which spelled my dog's name, but he was on a roll. Just as I was gathering the words to explain my plan for getting Lumpi into heaven, all hell broke loose, so to speak.

"This is disgraceful! A totally disgusting desecration of God's word. How *dare* you?" my father raged. Even my Mom sadly shook her head as she contemplated her little girl roasting in hell. I remember thinking, *Well, I am just a kid*, and it still made perfect sense to me to lay some solid groundwork to get the old boy into heaven; after all, Lumpi *did* eat the head off my Ginny doll.

As I watched my parents, stiff and straight, on the living room couch, I had a hard time imagining the Jesus on the rock, whose picture was hanging in my Sunday School room, blasting those little ones for putting their dogs' names in the front cover of their Bibles. But somehow this didn't seem like a good time to mention that, so I stood there and accepted the rage of my parents, and then I dutifully erased Lumpi's name, if ever so lightly . . . just in case . . .

In the sixth grade, I was invited to Jackie Saunder's birthday party and upon my arrival I met her dog – a Newfoundland. A giant teddy bear of a dog that was thrilled when I plopped down on the floor to rub his tummy. Jackie's mom asked me to join in the festivities, but there was no budging me. Jackie? I couldn't care less. I had no interest in sweets, games or the birthday girl, and instead spent the entire party down on the floor with the dog. While this decision made for a great afternoon, my lack of social graces meant I was never to be invited back to Jackie's house.

I dated a myriad of boys throughout high school and adhered to a strict policy of eight dates or eight weeks, whichever came first, and the guy was history. (Of course, there were a few guys with policies of their own who dumped me before I could dump them.) Then came college. The first person I met was Bill. He seemed interesting. Then, just prior to homecoming, Bill commented that he had gone to the corner deli to get himself a foot-long hoagie. As he headed back to campus, he stopped to eat the sandwich, which he also shared with the campus's stray mutt. This dog was considered a family friend by many kids and a campus pest by others. Bill not only liked this dog, he *shared his sandwich* with him and those sandwiches were gold to us college kids who had no money and were stuck living off cafeteria slop. Bill had his priorities straight. I knew I had to marry him.

I took Bill home to meet the family. Not the parents, but rather Lumpi. Being a good judge of character, Lumpi had already snapped at a few male guests, which indicated that a dumping was in order. How could I have a relationship if Lumpi did not approve?

Bill not only passed the test, he actually liked Lumpi, a reaction which was surprising because by this time, our chubby little dachshund was gray from head to foot, with filmy eyes and a raspy bark that unleashed a spray of bad breath that could set your hair on fire. Wedding plans were made.

After several years of marital bliss and a round of open-heart surgery, the biological clock was now free to tick-tick, which slowly began to sound more like a *gong-gong*. Time for kids. *Kids?* This meant assuming responsibility for another living thing. Could we do it? It seemed doubtful, so we decided on a plan – a test. We'd have a baby, but the four-legged kind. Then, if we were able to keep that kid alive for two years, we'd add a human.

Enter Sofe. After falling in love with our neighbor's black Lab, we found a breeder whose litter was born on our wedding anniversary: an omen that this child was meant to be. The runt was our new baby. Twenty-four hours after we cradled our baby in pink bunting to bring her home, she began to bleed when she went to the bathroom. In a panic, we rushed her to an emergency vet, paying double for his services because it was the Fourth of July. He quickly informed us, "Take her back. Get a new one." *What?* We had poured our love into this dog for 24 hours. A new one? Trade her in? It was all Bill could do to keep me from leaping over the examining table and choking this cold-hearted fool. Instead, we took home every medicine known to veterinarian science and maintained an all-night vigil at our baby's bedside.

The next day Bill had been planning to fly to see his folks, but with a sick child there was no way he could leave until the crisis passed. This meant that he had to turn his advance purchase ticket in for a much higher-priced one after Sofe made a remarkable recovery the next day. The financial commitment of parenthood was starting to show. Had a wooden thermometer been mounted on our front lawn to track the financial output we were investing in our child, its numbers would have rivaled the annual budget of some Third World countries.

But the financial commitment didn't end with medical expenses. Once Sofe regained her health, we found out she was one mischievous puppy. She had a tendency to eat things – like my $45 white European goose down pillow while Bill's $7 polyester fiberfill pillow lay untouched. But we understood the art of the kill. Sofe was a retriever, after all, and she was just looking for the duck.

The destruction of the couch was not as easy to accept. After rebuilding and upholstering an antique sofa, I came home one day to find it in little tiny pieces – itsy-bitsy little pieces – all over the living room. The only thing left was the wooden frame. It turns out my Italian upholsterer had used horsehair lining and, sure enough, Sofe was looking for the horse. We were impressed with her keen sense of smell.

When the upholsterer returned to redo the job he had just completed the week before, his mouth dropped open at what remained of his handiwork.

"Other than fire, I have never seen such destruction," he murmured as he carried the sofa back out to his truck.

"Just don't forget to leave the horse out this time," I called out as a reminder.

Then there was the neon yellow Playtex Living Glove. It was missing from my sink one morning, and the next day I noticed Sofe struggling to go to the bathroom. Sure enough, out of her butt came a human finger, bright yellow, showing no signs of its route through Sofe's digestive system. It was followed by another and yet another finger until an entire human hand slowly worked its way out. Amazing! Despite the fact that there was no damage to the glove, I decided it was time to purchase a whole new pair.

The next week Sofe sipped some wax stripper as I was redoing floors. About 30 minutes later she began to convulse as she vomited the contents of her stomach. Panicked, I called the local poison control to find out how to save my baby.

"I have this dog and . . ." I started in after the phone was picked up on the first ring.

"Please hold," was the curt answer.

Seconds turned to minutes as I realized these people just didn't understand, so I hung up and dialed again.

"My daughter just drank wax stripper." That got their attention. A physician was on the phone in a second.

"She's vomited all over the place but it seems to have slowed," I continued.

The doctor wanted all my daughter's details. Where was she now?

"Under the bed." I slipped.

"What?"

"She must be afraid. She does that sometimes," I countered, realizing this conversation was going to have to be carefully thought out.

"Ask her where it hurts."

"She can't talk," I stammered. I had no earthly clue whether 2-year-old humans could speak or not. Now my kid would have to have some kind of mental handicap, which probably more aptly applied to her mother.

Fortunately, the doctor never suspected a thing. Sofe vomited all of the poison out of her system, and poison control even called back later that evening to see how my little girl was doing. I just made sure that I answered the phone before Bill when it rang.

Next up was the year's supply of homemade preserves, which crash-landed into a gooey mess of glass shards on the basement floor after our baby tried to perch her ever-growing body on a shelf. Poor thing, Sofe must have been hungry.

To try and save our furnishings, we decided to place Sofe in the basement each morning as we headed off to work, where she would spend the day eating through the wall into our garage. Each night Bill would then reapply a new layer of plywood. We were becoming fast friends with the local lumber store guys.

One day I called out to Sofe as I arrived home expecting to find bits of plywood all over the basement. But the walls were in relatively good shape and she was nowhere to be found. The window tucked under the ceiling showed a gaping hole. Sofe had somehow jumped up onto the workbench and then over several feet and out the window! I raced outside expecting to find my baby dead on the grass, but instead she was sitting on the back deck with a gaping slice down her leg, happy to see I had finally made it home. A rush to the vet resulted in emergency surgery and several hundred more dollars added to our investment thermometer.

Sofe was showing signs she was lonely.

And all this lead to the disaster.

Our first Christmas as "parents" was spent at my folks' house. Two days later my sister was scheduled to fly home and the whole family decided to trek to the airport for our good-byes. However, my parents didn't have a specially reinforced basement in which to contain my mischievous baby.

"You're not leaving *that* dog here alone," my mother insisted as she eyed her couch with God only knows what kind of animal scent hidden inside.

"No problem. We'll take her with us." As proud parents, Bill and I loved to take our baby along and, as a rule, that wasn't a problem – except maybe the time we took Sofe to visit friends at an apartment with a strict No-Animals rule. We placed dark glasses on Bill, taped white paper around the shaft of his golf putter and headed off as Blind Man and Wife. Sofe, however, didn't know how to play this game and she proceeded to pull Bill into the bushes, wee-weeing on the flowers, causing all kinds of havoc. We made a mental note not to submit her name to the seeing-eye people and, interestingly, those friends became another family we were never invited back to visit.

"You can't take a dog into an airport," Mom continued.

"Don't worry, Mom, blind people do it all the time."

So, off we went, arriving at the main terminal along with hundreds of other holiday travelers laden down with gifts and luggage. My father dropped off the entire family, dog and all, at the curb while he headed to find a parking spot. We joined the holiday rush, gabbing and laughing as we headed indoors. The crowd funneled toward the escalators, which led everyone upstairs to the gates. I held Sofe close and we took our place in line. Just as it was my turn to step on the escalator, Sofe balked. What was this? She didn't like it, not one bit. So, as she dug her feet into the ground, refusing to budge, people behind us began to back up – grumbling and fussing about the jam. I pulled out of line with my family, wondering what to do next.

"It's OK." I needed to sound calm. Yes, that's it, sound calm. "Sofe just needs to see us move confidently and she'll get the hang of this," I said as we headed back to the end of the line. The crowd movement continued unabated, slowly working its way toward the escalator and immediately a steady stream of people stepped in behind us.

"Keep moving," I whispered to my mom and sister. "Just keep moving."

Sofe's turn at the escalator again caused a hesitation, but this time I was prepared. I tugged on her leash, giving her no choice but to step onto the moving stairs. Piece of cake. And we thought sweet little Sofe was going to give us trouble. Every step in front and behind us was filled with a person, suitcase or shopping bag filled with gifts.

As I stepped off the escalator, keeping with the flow, I felt a pull. Expecting Sofe to bound joyfully off the escalator, I looked back to find her hunched over doing her bathroom duty. That escalator had scared the crap out of my dog! And it was a haven't-gone-in-a-week-and-this-sure-feels-good one. A big one that was now being mashed into the floor as the escalator steps flattened out to complete their ride back downstairs. Sofe, not liking to walk and poop at the same time, remained firmly planted as people, luggage, and gifts continued to arrive in a steady stream.

That's when the screaming started. Screaming and leaping . . . lots and *lots* of screaming and leaping. For some reason, no one cared to step in the mess that waited at the escalator landing so, with no time to think, people began to scream and leap.

Scream and leap. Not a pretty picture, I might add, considering the number of out-of-shape travelers who just spent the holiday parked in a chair gorging on pecan pie.

My mother stood frozen in horror. My sister burst out laughing. I stared, glassy-eyed, at the crowd, which kept pouring up and off the escalator all the while mumbling, "Not my Sofe. She ain't done nuthin'. My Sofe . . . she's a goood girl. Not my Sofe. She ain't done nuthin' . . . "

Finally, an airport employee who raced over snapped me out of my stupor by sharing her feelings at the top of her lungs in a language I'm glad I didn't understand. I suspect she was not wishing me a happy holiday.

As with many traumatic events, where victims are sheltered from the horror with a form of situational amnesia, all I remember was that good-byes were short and sweet that year. But, as I said, I know it was not my fault, it was the disease – defective genes of a Black Lab Nut.

Icing on the Cake

"You have the results?" I stammered into the telephone.

"Yes, we do, Mrs. Wilson. It's positive."

"Positive? It *can't* be. Are you sure?"

"Yes, Mrs. Wilson, I'm sure. You're pregnant." The voice on the other end of the line sounded firm. It seemed doubtful that she could be talked out of this one.

"Oh my *God*, I thought it was the humidity..."

"The humidity? Now, Mrs. Wilson, it hasn't been *that* humid."

And thus, parenthood commenced. I was heavy with child or at least the heavy part lay sometime in the near future. Currently a microscopic blob-kid was floating around somewhere inside but it would evolve in due time into a thinking, feeling child. The concept bounced around my head, presenting all sorts of thoughts and possibilities and images.

I took a stab at pregnancy math. What month would this kid actually show up? What year would it enroll in kindergarten? Graduate from high school? If I, as the mother, baked a dozen bran muffins a week to assure the kid's regularity, how many muffins would I have to bake over the course of its lifetime? How many teaspoons of cinnamon would that require? Considering inflation, how much would have to be invested in cinnamon to fulfill the awesome responsibility of motherhood? For how long does this parenting thing require your utmost attention, anyway? Twenty-one years or was I off the hook after only 18? *Only* 18? Dogs were scary enough since they tended to hang around for 12 to 14 years. Eighteen years – that was way beyond my mental calendar.

The whole world changed with a simple dribble of pee in a paper cup. And that thought brought up another whole concern. Kids produce body by-products of their very own which of course represent one more responsibility that rests squarely on the shoulders of the poor mother who is already trying to keep up with the cinnamon thing. What would I do if I were totally incapable of dealing with body by-products? I had already been a miserable failure as a babysitter because of this very issue.

"We'd like you to baby-sit Little Johnny from 3 to 11 p.m.," the caller would say.

"No problem, as long as Little Johnny promises not to produce any poop, pee or barf during said hours." Needless to say, I didn't get a lot of takers for my services because Little Johnny's parents knew he was a virtual fountain of body by-products. As the mother I couldn't just make up some excuse and remove myself every time a diaper needed to be changed or throw-up needed to be dealt with. Eventually body by-products would have to be handled. My sister offered some encouragement: "God was real smart with this. The gross stuff starts out real small. This gives you time to adjust and then when it's no big deal, by-products increase." But my sister was a nurse; she *wallowed* in body by-products; body by-products were her *life*. Could she really be trusted that there would ever be a time when this would be no big deal?

Everything from here out was going to be different. My mind continued to explode with all the implications. Protect. I was now going to be responsible to keep some kid safe. Looking back on the number of near-death experiences Sofe our black Lab had logged while under my watchful eye, this was not going to be an easy undertaking. Teach. How was I going to teach someone things when there were way too many days when I didn't have enough brainpower for my own needs? What would happen now that I would be forced to share it? The positive side of this was the fact that when kids first show up they are in need of some serious teaching. Not even knowing they have toes, no less how to get the fuzz out from in between them, meant that I could somehow fake the *teach* category at least for a while. Entertain. This seemed the easiest of my upcoming new responsibilities. If I was lucky I could pass my love for Legos on to this kid, thereby having a valid excuse to get new and better sets – just as long as the kid realized from the start that he or she was not to get too close or to mix colors, resulting in tasteless creations. Love. I'd heard most parents really love their kids, even the ones with big noses and nasty dispositions. But then what about those teenage years? I'd never heard anything good about the teenage years. And looking back on my own stint in that era and my father's reactions to things I thought were no big deal presented a huge problem unless I could figure out a way to get the kid from adorable tike to self-supporting adult without going through the teenage years. I would have to put that worry on hold for some future time because taking all this in was way too much for me at the moment.

 First, I needed to focus. One worry at a time. This was not just some kid, this was my kid, The Kid. I needed to get a grip. Baby steps, that's it, I'd take baby steps with the baby. First I'd focus on protect. I needed to get The Kid home safe and sound since *we* were at work when the official word came in. This meant I'd have to somehow drive *us* the entire six miles without causing any serious harm or disability to The Kid. Parenthood was already way too much and I'd only been at it for 20 minutes. I needed to keep things in perspective. I'd give it 11 years. Eleven years seemed like a decent effort. The Kid should be out of diapers by then and might even be saying a word or two. Yeah, by eleven years I should get the hang of it.

As my toes disappeared under the moon-like sphere of my belly, I decided that not only would I accept the challenge of motherhood, I would embrace it and everything it entailed. I was going to be The Perfect Mother. My home would be immaculate, my kid would be immaculate. Martha Stewart would look like an incapable sloth compared to the perfect world I was going to create and oversee.

I took an inventory of areas where I lacked the necessary skill to function at such a high standard. A glaring deficiency immediately jumped out: I had no knowledge or skill in decorating cakes. How could I possibly call myself a mother if every annual celebration of my child's birth resulted in a mound of sticky, gooey slop adorned with the appropriate number of candles being placed in front of my kid? Surely this would result in low self-esteem and all its inherent side effects such as drug use, promiscuity, and poor grades, if my child would even choose to stay in school at all. I realized if I was lucky I had just enough time to eliminate this obvious sign of poor mothering – I had one year plus the remainder of my pregnancy in order to master the art of producing delicious, designer cakes.

A quick Yellow Page search revealed a shop dedicated to all things cake was located in the town next to mine. I wondered what that meant, since it wasn't a bakery but rather was an institution of "higher cake learning." As soon as I arrived, I marveled at just how deficient my knowledge was. The shop was filled to the rafters with cake stuff: decorative trinkets and tools, instruction manuals, ingredients from tiny bottles of flavoring to huge sacks of flour, and pans in every conceivable shape and size.

I had naïvely assumed that my cake-decorating skills would be used once a year for my kid's birthday celebrations, but no – the shop owner informed me that if I were to truly fulfill my maternal obligations, I would bake and decorate ground-hog cakes to usher in early February, rabbit cakes on Easter, flag-shaped cakes in July, turkey cakes to add a special festiveness to the Thanksgiving dinner, and of course, not to be forgotten, the ghost cake for Halloween. And this was only the start. As I stood at the owner's side, I followed her gaze as she lifted her eyes skyward, and with a sweeping gesture of her arm, she stated, "The sky's limit, you only must believe . . . believe in yourself, believe in the beauty of your creations and ultimately you will be hard-pressed to ignore all the cake-baking opportunities that can fill your days."

"Yes, I believe. I BELIEVE!" was all I could pant.

It was difficult to decide where to start. I decided to purchase the most basic gear: tubes, tips, and cake forms to launch me in my new adventure. Added to that was the first of many manuals, which spelled out simple decorating techniques. Beginner's lessons, held in a classroom in the back of the shop, would commence the following week. The interim would be spent reading and learning basic terminology in order to be able to keep up with the class. My kid was depending on it.

The first decorating class finally arrived. "Okay, ladies," our instructor opened. "We've got a lot of material to cover today and the only way to excel at decorating is to practice, practice, PRACTICE. Today we're going to cover basic buttercream icing." With that, our instructor placed an industrial-size vat on the table and ladled spoonfuls of pure white cream into a bowl. "Start by taking your solid vegetable shortening and add to it . . ."

"What's that," I whispered to the student next to me.

"That? That's shortening."

"Gee, it sure looks like Crisco," I continued out of the side of my mouth.

"Well it's *solid vegetable shortening – and that's what Crisco is*," the woman whispered back without taking her eyes off our instructor.

"But isn't Crisco for frying chicken?"

"Well, yeah. You fry chicken in it, too."

"So, does that mean someone expects us to *eat* chicken-frying Crisco?"

"Of *course* we're going to eat it, it's our buttercream icing," my neighbor hissed.

"Yeah, but if it's supposed to be *butter*cream icing, where's the butter?" And with that our teacher sprinkled two drops of butter-flavored extract into the large bowl of something that looked an awful lot like the stuff you fry your chicken in. Fake chemical butter in chicken grease – the makings of pure white icing. I sat in horror.

"I don't think I can eat that," I mumbled, and with that my neighbor's hand shot up in the air as she called out, "Could I come get a closer look?" And she was gone. I somehow suspected my questions were weighing heavily on my neighbor's own dreams to become the Perfect Cake-Decorating Mother.

Icing, the food that is synonymous with heaven for any kid and most adults when broken down into its most primitive parts was made of two things I had no desire to consume. But then, as the instructor finished whipping the smooth creamy product, we were all encouraged to take a taste. It was delicious, as good as any icing I've ever eaten, and better than most. If I was going to be The Perfect Mother, I'd just have to avoid focusing on the basics.

My homework assignment was to whip up a batch of this very same icing every day in order to be able to "play with it" – become familiar with the feel, the way it swirled, peaked, and held its shape. Using my newly purchased spatula, I was to become one with my icing. The second week we would move on to more elaborate piping and molding techniques. And so it went.

By week three, we were instructed to apply our new skills to real cakes.

"Bake, bake, BAKE!" our teacher charged.

"Why the cake?" Bill asked the next day.

"I've got to practice my basket weave."

"Who's it for?" he continued.

"Us." I hadn't really thought about who would eat all my homework assignments now that I would be making several cakes a week in order to develop icing expertise.

"Yeah, but what's that?"

"That? It's solid vegetable shortening," I mumbled.

"Solid vegetable shortening? You mean chicken-frying grease?"

A trend was started, a trend in my elusive quest to become The Perfect Mother. It began by identifying a shortcoming, translating it into a need, investing hundreds of dollars and thousands of hours to master a skill to serve this need, only to find that ultimately I and my family were better off in the first place, better off with Schlock Mom. Weeks and weeks of daily cake decorating and the inherent challenge of disposing of my homework assignments came to a screeching halt when local organizations, institutions, and neighbors eventually refused to open their doors to me, knowing that I was delivering one more unwanted confection. It was then that I was forced to ask myself, "So, what's really so bad about bakery cakes?" But sadly, a lasting lesson was not learned as cake decorating was quickly replaced with stenciling, croissant baking, rug braiding, furniture refinishing, appliquéing, and eventually English Cottage gardening.

Once a Yankee, Always a Yankee

The corporate dictate came in the summer of 1987. *Thou shalt move to Atlanta.* Atlanta? Could this possibly be true? A born-and-bred Yankee who had bounced back and forth between Northeast and Midwest, I was now getting my first shot as being Southern, *genteeeel* Southern. I was thrilled, but at the same time I suspected the Southerners were not going to be half as excited with my arrival.

My most recent foray into the South had come when, as Bill's wife, I was invited to Richmond to wine and dine some of my husband's best clients. I remembered visiting Virginia as a child with my family on a *this is your country; experience it* trip, and it seemed like an easy drive from New York. I thought Virginia was one of us. So, wanting to clarify this impression, I got everyone's attention at Bill's company's final gala and politely asked, "Now, do you Virginians consider yourself part of the North or part of the South?" The world stopped. My husband glared at me from across the room with such a look I knew he was at that moment recalculating the annual projected income he could expect from this region — from lots to zip. I knew now they were part of the South.

So, not wishing to stir up old wounds — my husband's as well as the Southerners' — I decided to get myself an education. A friend of mine who had spent some time in the South told me I just *had* to get this magazine called *Southern Living*. This was going to be my bible. Now *this* was my kind of education.

I read it faithfully. I learned all the terms like "y'all" and "huush." I bought a box of grits and kept it in the cabinet, just in case.

I was ready to make the move except for one thing. My wisdom teeth desperately needed to come out. I'd known this for a mere 10 years, but now, unsure if dentists in the South were into pain, I decided to take last-minute advantage of a highly credentialed dentist who looked like a fire hydrant, sounded like a government spy from a Third World country, but had a reputation for pain-free dentistry. I had, so far, trusted him with cleaning my teeth. At every previous visit, he had assured me that he not only pulled the teeth of paranoid patients, he *loved* pulling the teeth of paranoid patients (i.e., he loved me). So as my good-bye gift, I decided to let him pull my teeth.

The day before Moving Day, I popped a few pills that my pain-free dentist had given me as a minor pre-pulling sedative.

"Just make sure you don't drive," I was instructed.

The cabby pulled up to my house, and as I slipped into the back seat, I realized this hairy little fellow with the chipped tooth and the twitch in his right eye was one of the most beautiful human beings I had ever seen. I suspected I was falling in love. We drove past the local landfill, which now appeared in all its glory as majestic as any mountain range. It was beautiful; all the world was beautiful. I made a mental note to ask my dentist for a few extras of those little pills just in case I'd have a bad day tomorrow or any day for that matter.

"You know, he could take care of that tooth for you . . ." I called out to my new best-friend cabby as he pulled away from the curb. He smiled a big chipped-tooth smile over whatever I had just tipped this perfect specimen of a human. My math stinks on a clear day and I had probably rewarded him with a down payment on a Harley or maybe even a double-wide.

"Drive careful, my friend . . ." I wasn't sure if he winked back at me or if it was just that old twitch kicking in again.

And the love didn't end there. I loved the receptionist, I loved the office décor, the dental aroma, the melodic whizzing of a drill coming from the back room. I especially loved my spy-dentist. I loved the whole experience of hearing my teeth being ripped from the back of my skull. It was a happy day, a very happy one indeed.

The next day I was back to reality. My gums ached. I had gaping holes where my molars had been and I was forced to sip liquids through a straw as the movers carried box after box out to the truck. Darah, having said good-bye to her kindergarten playmates, decided to entertain herself by seeing how fast she could run up the ramp that was secured to the back of the moving truck. Instead of arriving with lightning speed in the empty cavern of the truck, she landed flat on her face, splat on the ramp. The surface, which provided great traction for moving men with large boxes, was also was great for ripping the skin off little 5-year-old faces. Now two of us were not happy. Where had all the love gone? I wondered.

The plan was for the moving van to leave ahead of us while we stayed behind to clean the empty house and then load up the dogs, the kids, the vacuum and drive down to meet them.

"OK, lady, take one last look."

"Naw, zat's O-hay, oo ott 'erehing," I garbled through wads of cotton still padding the back of my throat. "Zee oo in a 'ouple o' 'ays." With that, the truck lumbered away from the curb in a southerly direction.

"What's this?" Bill asked just moments after the moving van pulled away as we stepped into what was supposed to be a vacant master bedroom. A very large box sitting innocently in the center of the room meant our leisurely trip in an SUV was now going to resemble something more like a troupe of clowns stuffed in a VW beetle. All I could do was smile a big bulging smile and shrug. Oh, well, at least it couldn't get worse.

Exhausted, we feasted on peanut butter sandwiches and then we set up camp on Darah's bedroom floor so we could get an early start on scrubbing before we headed out the next afternoon.

Suddenly, out of a sound sleep, I sat bolt upright in my sleeping bag. Something was not right. There were funny sounds coming from my stomach, and it seemed that the peanut butter sandwich was no longer welcome. I decided to make a quick visit to the bathroom and while there I found out just how unhappy my stomach was and how unwelcome the peanut butter sandwich was. I also found out how the gaping holes in the back of my throat were a convenient stopping ground for my unwelcome supper. I headed back to camp, but what seemed like only moments later, a second trip to the bathroom was necessary and a third and fourth and on and on. By the fifth trip I was no longer heading back to camp. All I could manage was to crawl on all fours as my energy was being flushed down the toilet in the form of The Flu of a Lifetime.

When the sun finally spilled through the windows and Bill and the kids woke, I was sprawled out on the rug as far from camp as I could get for fear that I might breathe flu-breath on one of them. The last thing we needed was another sick person — I was sick enough for all four of us.

"What are you doing over here?" Bill asked as he peered down at my limp body next to the closet.

"I'm dead."

"Dead?"

"Yes, dead . . . I spent the night draped over the toilet . . . you see my toes? They're hollow. When my stomach couldn't find anything more to throw up, it sucked out toe meat."

"You threw up toe meat?"

"Only after I picked it out of those stupid-ass holes in my gums . . . go away . . . "

With that Bill announced to the kids they were going to learn a new game called *Cleaning House,* and he kindly steered them downstairs to do the work we were supposed to have done together.

A short time later Bill rushed back into the room, "Rudy — get up. *Hurry* . . . get up. Look your perky best — we've got COMPANY."

"Go away . . . or you'll find toe meat on your shoes."

"No, no . . . you can't lie here." Bill stood over me with his arms flapping like a little sparrow attempting his first flight. "There's a *Realtor* coming. GET UP. *People* want to look at the *house.*"

"I don't care . . . I threw up toe meat for God's sake."

My philosophical husband had always maintained that it took only one buyer to sell a house, but right now my throbbing head told me this was not going to be the one. Bill was not willing to give up quite so easily, so he straddled what was left of my body, cupped his hands under my armpits, and dragged me away from full view of our soon-to-be guests, i.e. into the empty closet.

"All right . . . now . . . just make sure you don't get up," he ordered as he switched off the light.

"Refresh my memory, how much education do we have between the two of us?" I mumbled as he gently closed the door. I could hear voices downstairs and an exceptionally cheerful Bill as he attempted to steer these potential buyers anywhere but to the closet that now held his half-dead wife propped against the back wall.

"Oh, my . . . "

"Ahhh . . . I'd like you to meet my wife . . . she's been feeling a little under the weather."

"Hey, look, it's *Mommy*. Mommy? . . . What are you doing in the closet, Mommy?" Darah's voice chimed in as she peeked from between the adults' legs.

I waved up at all the nice people who had gathered and were now peering into the closet to get a better look at the lifeless mound slumped on the floor. Needless to say, there wasn't a lot of small talk as the Realtor and her charges decided it was time to move on, and just as I had predicted, these were in fact not THE buyers.

After Bill cheerfully wished them well, he returned to sit next to me in the closet with a look I had seen before. It said *give this moment some time to process, to ferment — and it may take years — but one day we will look back at this and laugh*. Somehow the two of us were very good at creating these kinds of moments.

Later that afternoon, with rooms cleaned, Bill loaded the kids, the dogs, the vacuum, and that stupid box that was supposed to be on the moving van into the car for our trek south. I curled up on the front seat to continue my recuperation.

The following morning we stopped at a roadside café for breakfast. As I picked at a piece of toast, a very large trucker wolfed down an unbelievably inordinate amount of food. Upon finishing, he sauntered up to the waitress, wrapped his big, brawny arms around her and cooed, "Have a g'day babe." Brad, watching the two, asked, "Daddy, what's ag'daybabe?" We had arrived. Welcome to the South.

The next day as our possessions were being unloaded from the moving van, a lady named Tina made her way over from next door with homemade chocolate chip cookies that were still warm from the oven — Southern hospitality at its very best. After we finished inhaling the cookies, I had Darah return the tin to Tina with our thanks.

Upon returning, Darah burst in the door and said, "Mom, you won't *believe* this. Tina was just sitting on the couch — not going ANYWHERE — and she had LIPSTICK on." I made a mental note — wear more lipstick.

By now, Christmas was fast approaching. My *Southern Living* bible instructed me that holidays were not complete without magnolia leaves. They needed to be everywhere, on the table, draped from the hallway. *Everywhere.* Three big, beautiful magnolia trees were perched on a hill, next to Tina's house, overlooking my driveway. I wondered if I dared ask to borrow a few leaves for my decorations. No, that would be too easy, so under cover of darkness with stealth-like swiftness I helped myself to what I needed. I tiptoed ever so gently to make sure Tina and her husband were not alerted to my mission. I carefully "borrowed" equally from each of the three trees, and, as a result, the holiday proceeded with decorative grandeur.

As our second Southern Christmas rolled around, I was still not able to ask for magnolia leaves, so I once again donned my darkest clothes and helped myself.

Then, after the third Christmas, festering guilt, hidden deep in my bowels, seemed to burst forth like a bubble. "Tina . . . I must confess . . . every Christmas I steal your magnolia leaves . . . I'm really sorry, even though it probably doesn't seem that way since I've been doing it for three years now and you'd think I'd somehow find a way to ASK but NOOOO. It's to do my best Southern decorations, which, by the way, are much more festive than anything those *Yanks* could ever come up with and I've been very diligent about not creating any horticultural holes so as to diminish the value and exceptional beauty of your trees, I hope you'll understand and . . . please, forgive me."

Tina looked at me long and slow, as she tended to do, her head cocked in bewilderment as my confession sunk in. Then she stated softly, with perfectly painted lips, "Hun-ney, those are y'aaaall's magnolias!"

Say what? *My* magnolias? Mine? I'd been wracked with guilt over stealing my *own* magnolia leaves. Oh, well, once a Yankee, always a Yankee.

When the company required that we return north to our homeland in 1994, we stated in the sales contract of our house: P.S. The magnolias are yours.

To Trust a Clever Canary

"Mommy, Josh's daddy is sick." Darah shared this tidbit of news as she downed her after-school snack.

Standing at the kitchen sink, I commented half-heartedly, "Oh, really, does he have a cold or the flu?" These two conditions seemed to fit the gamut of possible illnesses.

"No, he has cancer," she stated, surely not able to grasp the significance of this disease, to which I felt proudly immune.

Joshua was an adorable boy with white-blond hair who lived down the street from the house we had moved into just months earlier. Even though he passed through my kitchen regularly, I had never met his parents. A sudden deep dread filled me as I anticipated that time. What would I say? "I'm sorry"?

Lists of cancer risks were occasionally included in related newspaper articles, and as I would cautiously peruse the information, I was thankful that I and the people I loved the most were not candidates.

Bill and I were not smokers, we filtered our water, and we never lived on top of a toxic dump. We even ate broccoli regularly and, amazingly, we had no history of cancer on either side of our families. But now this disease had invaded my world through the casual friendship of my daughter's kindergarten playmate.

My first instinct was to step forward and offer help. But how? Contemplating a life-threatening disease of any of my loved ones was beyond my ability. God gives us only what we can handle, my beliefs told me, and God certainly knew this one was way out of my league. Besides, there had to be some sort of system in place where you earned points – crisis credits – that would make you ineligible for any further medical suffering. But that still left the dilemma of how I was to relate to Josh's mom and dad.

I remembered back to the time when I faced my own surgery. Friends and acquaintances were quick to *ooh* and *aah* at the prospect. Occasionally people shared stories of a favorite uncle who had undergone this risky procedure, "God rest his soul." Each encounter seemed to knock me down a peg psychologically, even though doctors had assured me of a full recovery. Now I visualized myself as these well-meaning people, stumbling over my own tongue and surely saying the wrong thing.

I asked my pastor, "What do I do?"

"Why don't you just be yourself," he suggested.

"Are you crazy? I can't do that."

The most logical alternative was to provide stealth support. I encouraged Darah to make plans with young Joshua, thus giving a break to his parents, and enabling me to carefully avoid any communication with his family.

Once as I was returning Josh to his house, I pulled into the driveway just as a lady I assumed to be his mother pushed a wheelchair from the side of a car. A slight man with wisps of white hair on both sides of his head sat hunched over. The man turned and slowly looked in our direction.

"Is that your grandpa?" Darah cheerfully asked.

"No, that's my dad," Josh answered slowly. As my daughter grasped that fact she added without any apparent hesitation or surprise, "Well, he looks like a very nice man."

"Yes, he is," Josh assured us. I wondered how my daughter was blessed with such panache when all I could do at that moment was to meekly wave to the couple.

In only a matter of weeks, word spread that Joshua's dad lost his battle with cancer. I respectfully left his family alone in its time of grief. Within the year, Joshua and his mom moved to another state to be closer to family. My experience with cancer was done.

Done, that is, until one morning in October, six years later. It was a dreary Saturday morning. A tap on my shoulder and Bill immediately pointed to a lump on his neck.

"Hey, look at this. What do you think it is?"

"That? Looks like swollen glands," I mumbled, too sleepy to launch into a conversation of any significance.

"Swollen glands? Aren't glands under the ears?" Bill questioned.

"Nah, they can show up anywhere. Ears to the elbows. Depends a lot on atmospheric pressure," I suggested, trying to buy more quiet time.

But Bill wasn't convinced. He wanted to see a doctor. I was skeptical. First, I maintained a policy that any lump or bump should be grapefruit size before being checked out. Also, Bill didn't have a good history with doctor visits. Years earlier, bothered by a rash on his neck, Bill had scheduled an appointment with a dermatologist he found through the Yellow Pages. The dermatologist's office was in a high rise on Chicago's Magnificent Mile, not far from Bill's office. Upon arriving, he was ushered into one of the most spectacular offices he had seen, complete with lush Oriental rugs and bookshelves of rich mahogany. As he sat on the leather couch, he marveled at how dermatology must be very lucrative if the surroundings were any indication. When the doctor arrived, he sat opposite Bill in a wing chair, crossing his legs, obviously in no rush.

"So how are you doing today?"

"Well, I guess, fine overall."

"You guess? So things aren't really all that fine?"

"Well, no, there is this one problem."

"Yes, go on, please."

"Well it's this rash," Bill continued as he pulled his collar from his neck.

"I see. And how do you *feel* about having a rash?"

"How do I feel? Well, I guess you could say . . . itchy," Bill offered.

"And does it bother you, having this itch?" the doctor continued to probe.

That's when bells and whistles began chiming in. Bill's head, a virtual concert of *Do you really FEEL this is appropriate, dermatologically speaking?* So Bill decided to get right to the point, "Can you give me something for this rash? I'm on my lunch hour . . ."

"You mean the rash really does itch?" the doctor stumbled. "You aren't here for a psychiatric session?"

"Well, if I stay here much longer, I might take you up on that offer." Finally, the two bewildered guys put their heads together and decided that Bill must have misdialed when making the appointment. It told me that Bill was not to be trusted within the medical community. *Sick* was clearly my area of expertise.

But something told Bill this pea sitting on his shoulder warranted attention. Monday morning and a visit to a doctor confirmed that the lump was not a problem. Then, two weeks later, it was still there, so a biopsy was scheduled – just to be on the safe side.

"Well, it's cancer," the surgeon announced as he strode up to my chair in the middle of the hospital waiting room. The words echoed in my ears. This was not possible. What about all the years of broccoli eating? What about my open-heart surgery? Didn't that earn us the right to be crisis-free from here on out? Without a moment's warning or preparation, when all seemed to be going according to plan in our lives, I had been sucked into the shoes of Joshua's mom.

The surgeon continued to describe what lay ahead, which wasn't much of anything until the lab results were all in.

"I can't handle this," I whispered. *Yeah, that's it. Declare your unwillingness to accept this. Make it known, fight it, protest, and it will all go away.*

The surgeon glanced down at his watch; probably another patient was being prepped for his skillful hand, so he cradled my elbow and whisked me to a nearby office.

"I need this room," he informed the occupant, and with that the woman sitting at the desk obediently got up and walked out. *She must know. I'll bet she can just guess it's cancer,* I thought as she stepped around my zombie-like body standing on the threshold of the office

I was about to take over. The surgeon's role was over. He clearly had other needs to attend to, and I was not being the understanding, strong spouse, anxious to move forward with an aggressive campaign to lick this problem.

"Get over it," he stated as he headed toward the door. "You've got no choice. Besides, I've had cancer and I beat it." With that he was gone. I lay my hand over the phone on the desk and somehow my fingers dialed a number that I didn't even realize was stored in my memory. As I muttered the words, "It's cancer," my pastor dropped everything and came to my side. He sat with me and held my hand. He didn't say a lot because I did enough babbling for both of us. He was just there and that was exactly what I needed. It was what I had been unable to do for Joshua's mom.

An aggressive course of radiation was the best option for treatment. As the holidays approached, Bill and I promised each other that our next year was going to be a better one. Then just as the New Year began, Bill's company announced it wanted him to return to the home office. Move? We conferred with Bill's doctors and they assured us we were dealing with a non-aggressive, slow-growing cancer. We needed to get on with our lives.

It was late the next summer that the moving van finally delivered us to our new home. Home, sweet home, a new adventure awaited.

But a short time later our new adventure consisted of daily trips to Boston's Dana Farber Cancer Institute after Bill started having trouble digesting food. Doctors kept scratching their heads as they poked and prodded to locate the invisible enemy, a cancer that could not even be pinpointed. Meanwhile, Bill kept losing weight. Out of respect and sympathy and sheer terror my body decided, *well if he can't digest, I won't either.* It seemed almost sacrilegious to enjoy food that my best friend in the world could not. By Thanksgiving, doctors decided to insert a catheter in Bill's neck to bypass the digestive system and instead intravenously feed him a bag of white gooey nutrients. "Umm, turkey in a bag," our 10-year-old son Brad summized as he poked at the bag of goo.

"You know, there's something I need to tell you," Bill started slowly.

"I love you," I whispered, trying to keep Bill from going further.

"Yes, I love you too, but there's more. I'm afraid . . ." I didn't want to go down this road. This was a conversation meant for the movies. A conversation when the hero says all the things that need to be said and you, a third-party observer with popcorn in hand, feel your throat tie into a knot and your heart pounds with dread and tears fill your eyes. And even as you murmur over and over, "This guy's okay, really he's okay. Remember it's only a movie, you saw him last Tuesday on late-night TV. *Really.* He's okay."

"Please, Bill..."

"No, I have to. I have to tell you something. I'm afraid. I'm afraid if something happens to me . . . you'll . . . you'll never remember to change the oil."

"Oil? Like in the car's engine kind of oil? You're worried about me changing the oil?"

"Yes. I know you're just not the type."

"Well, now that you mentioned it," I agreed. Bill had a point. I wasn't an oil changer. "Would you feel better if I promised never to run out of oil?" I asked as I brushed the hair from his forehead.

"Yes, but take it one step further, punk – change it long before you run out. Promise?"

"Promise." That was it. When the love you share with someone permeates every cell in your being each and every day of your life and "I love you" declarations are as comfortable and common as "please pass the salt," then your ultimate "I know our time together is limited" conversation can take a whole new twist.

With the catheter inserted, Bill was sent home to get some rest and gain some weight. The ever-elusive cancer would be addressed after the New Year. This plan lasted two days.

"Get him to the hospital," were the instructions after I called to report a night of vomiting, which spells trouble for someone on IV nutrients.

Upon our arrival at the hospital, the decision was made to operate. Doctors needed to open Bill up to see what was going on. As soon as the doctor walked into the waiting room, his eyes said it all. No words were necessary. Cancer was having a field day inside Bill's gut.

A nurse came by and slipped a piece of cardboard into my hand. As Bill was coming out of anesthesia he signaled that he wanted to write a note, scratched out in pencil, and addressed to the kids. It told of his love, it told of his pride, it ended with, "trust a clever canary."

Trust a clever canary. I read it over and over to see if somehow through a process of mental fermentation it would make sense. Finally, I presented the note back to Bill, "Hey, nice note, but what's with the bird?" He slowly read it out loud. "I remember writing it, but I don't have a clue. All I can guess is one day God will give you your canary."

Six days later God called Bill home.

Automatic pilot took over. The only means of functioning was to take tiny baby steps. *Swing your legs over the side of the bed, now stand, put one foot in front of the other, turn right, go down the stairs, the kids need breakfast.*

People, mostly strangers, seemed to come out of the woodwork with offers of help. And as our family's loss became known, people would show up at our door with donated food. Lasagnas, lots and lots of lasagnas.

As the weeks passed and more people asked, *What happened?* I decided to write a single letter describing the first three months in our new home. Reading back the words on the paper opened an emotional pit. There it was, spelled out in black and white: Bill died, I was a widow, a single parent. Emotions that had been building burst forth with such powerful sobs that even breathing was nearly impossible.

Finally, after what seemed like hours, the well of tears deep within me began to dry. I realized I needed to do something physical to move past the pain. An exercise bike sat in the sunroom overlooking our yard. I decided to ride until the physical pain of exhaustion hurt more than the pain in my heart. A book sat on the bike rack, unread for all the months we had been in our new home. I slowly pushed the pedals, knowing that it could be hours before some sort of wholeness was restored.

As beads of sweat began to pearl along the edge of my forehead, I opened the book to where the marker said I had last left off. The book was about power. Power that God can provide – if you'll only let Him. The author wrote of a man who lost his wife and two children when their home burned down. Then years later, instead of being consumed by rage and sorrow, this man, a songwriter, wrote and sang songs of praise to God, a God who I suspected had made some terrible mistake. Then words began to jump off the page. Tender words yet with a power I had never felt before: "Golden sunlight streamed into the room spotlighting the face of the singer. As he sang, a canary in a cage above the piano also began to sing. Man and bird seemed in perfect attunement as together they poured forth praise to the Lord who gives overcoming power to human beings. And who knows? Perhaps to birds also."

A canary. My canary. It was whispering, *hold on, trust, you are not alone.*

I got off the bike and had a pretty good day.

This Must Be Love

Anyone who has ever fallen in love knows that this phenomenon typically reveals itself in a significant moment or perhaps a series of moments when, all of a sudden, you stop and say, "this must really be love."

With Bill, I experienced this revelation at 2 a.m. on the 3rd of August 1973. It was then that I barfed into my plastic roller bag, the only moisture-proof container I could find, while huddled in my aunt's attic guest room. The source of my malady was the excited anticipation of hearing Bill's voice for the first time in the three months I was on a summer visit to Germany. The last thing he had said to me as I boarded the plane was, "I'll call you on your birthday." While Bill was never moved to vomit (a shortcoming I wondered about over the years), it was during his birthday phone call that he asked, "Will you marry me?" This combined with a squishy roller bag was enough to suggest true love.

I again experienced a this-must-be-love moment on the afternoon of March 2, 1996. A birthday once again, only this time it was my son's 12th birthday. It was *supposed* to be the day Brad would launch his dating career, which was a mature and sophisticated way of saying he would be delivered to the cinema by his mommy at a time synchronized with a person of the opposite sex who would arrive in her own mommy's mini-van in order to share a double-butter popcorn in the front row of a G-rated matinee. Sucking face in the back row does not typically occur for several more months for most 12-year-olds.

Instead, this day arrived with a freak snowstorm producing blizzard-like conditions, and it evolved into a day that Brad, even many years later, is unable to recall without breaking into a nervous twitch. It was a day he categorizes as one of a handful of black days when he realized that, unlike other children with normal, sane parents, he is stuck with the likes of me. And this was the day I realized, once again, that I was in love.

For the previous two months, I had been in a quandary as to what to do about a guy named Mike. While I felt all along Mike was special, he had a huge drawback that made our future together doubtful. Mike did not possess a bulbous nose encrusted with rose-colored warts, ending in two nostrils filled with protruding nose hairs from which a constant drip of mucus appeared. I somehow think I could have dealt with that. No, Mike's problem was something much worse and socially embarrassing – it was his car. A station wagon in an era when station wagons had gone the way of dinosaurs and ice boxes, it was a car that should have been put to rest many, many, *many* miles earlier. This car's door, at least the one that would open at all, would squeal and crunch and groan as you pulled up on it with all your strength to realign it into the hole the manufacturer had originally intended for it to occupy, back in the days when it had a handle and a solid rust-and-corrosion-free veneer. Had the producers of the Beverly Hillbillies needed a vehicle with a roof, this was their car. In other words, it was the ugliest car on the face of the earth, and Mike loved it.

I asked God what we should do about this problem. I suspected He wasn't keen on the concept of judging people based on their mode of transportation, but I just couldn't get over the profound ugliness. I suggested that God get rid of it – always with a quick reminder that no one should get hurt, a thoughtful gesture to help sway the scales toward "Sweet Rudy" rather than "Evil Rudy." Because I figured Mike was not the kind of person who was going to wake up one day and smell the ugly, I knew if there was to be any future to our relationship, this car would have to experience a catastrophic demise.

Theft, yes, that's an idea. The only problem was no thief in his right mind would have anything to do with this car. Even transporting the car to the slums of Mexico for a quick sale would result in screams of horror and disgust from folks whose abodes consist of scraps of wood and cardboard. "¿Usted está loco estúpido? Este coche es un stinko verdadero."

Hoping the car would be stolen for parts was also ridiculous because the thing was so old and the few parts that had stubbornly refused to fall off were so rusted and corroded that resale was out of the question. No, a more creative means of elimination would have to occur, and what did finally unfold on this cold and blustery day in March was beyond anything I or any Hollywood producer could have conjured up.

A forecast of snow showers, which meant a dusting in our neck of New England, quickly turned to thick, heavy flakes falling with such intensity that our yard took on the appearance of a Currier and Ives winter wonderland. Not a problem for anyone able to light a fire and sip hot chocolate while curled up with a book, but our family had plans and things to do. Our church had invited a pastor from Boston to come down as guest preacher. This was a man every inch of five foot three who had fled the ravages of civil war in Liberia and who had been brought to the U.S. along with his family, resulting in a tear-jerker of a story. His incredible charm, wit, and wisdom endeared Mike and I through a chance friendship. Not only was this gentleman going to be a guest in my home, but we had invited the entire church to a brunch at my house following the next day's service. Plan A for today included Mike's helping me in the preparations for Sunday brunch prior to his heading to Boston to pick up his preacher friend. In the meantime, I would buzz Brad over to the movies for his hot date and then head to the bakery for some tasty treats to serve at brunch the next day. With the snow showing no signs of letting up and the roads quickly becoming impassable, it was crazy and dangerous for Mike to make the trip north in his ugly station wagon.

I owned two cars — a Trooper SUV and a Beemer sports car. The obvious choice of vehicle for making the trip safely to Boston was the SUV.

"Please take the Trooper," I urged Mike.

"No, you need to go out, too."

"Mike, the roads are horrible. You've got to use the four-wheel drive," I insisted.

"You mean it? You really don't mind?" he stammered. "Well, if you insist . . ." and then, he lovingly cradled my elbows as he leaned up against me to whisper, "but then you *have* to take my car to town. It'll handle the snow much better than the Beemer."

Say what? Your car? THE car? The car I couldn't be seen in, no less DRIVE? I had visions of the "girls of East Greenwich," women who donned diamonds and fur-lined warm-up suits to chat at the local coffee shop, peering out at the poor thing forced to drive by in a car that had obviously fallen off the heap of the local junkyard. "Rudy? Did you see that? Was that Rudy in that clunker?" they would whisper. How could I face my neighbors, the few new friends I had made since my arrival? Was it possible to drive a vehicle without showing one's head above the dash where an AM radio had been many years before?

After many visits to my sister in southern Florida, I knew there were senior citizens who had mastered driving while lying flat on their backs, or so it seemed, since no sign of a living creature could be seen through the windows. That would be me. This was going to work. It was going to be fine.

But how was I going to break the news to Brad? A boy whose favorite pastime with his dad had been test-driving Ferraris was going on his first date in a car that probably would have failed a test drive for a demolition derby.

"Well . . . if you insist." I smiled weakly back at Mike as I held my stomach hoping my next move would not be to throw up on his shoes – the sick kind of throw up, not to be confused with the love kind.

"Brad, dear," I began.

"All right, what's going on?" The IQ test we had ordered for Brad years earlier did not lie. While Bill and I thought Brad was doing poorly academically in the second grade, it turned out in fact he was a real sharp kid who just chose to entertain his fellow classmates in the back of the room rather than learn boring things like reading, writing, and arithmetic.

"You're not going to make me cancel the movies, are you?" Brad continued suspiciously.

"Why no, not at all . . . dear. You're still going to go."

"Okay, then why do you look so weird?"

"Weird? Me? Weird? What makes you say that?"

"Mom, give it to me straight. Something's up," my highly intuitive kid insisted.

"Well, funny you should ask . . . but, it's been decided that Mike is going to drive the Trooper to Boston, which is by far the best option in this weather, which I'm sure you understand and are just fine about. Aaand . . . we're going to take his car, since that'll handle the roads better than the Beemer, which is also just fine. Besides, there will be so few cars out in this weather, it'll be fine, just . . . fine . . . really. Fine. . ." I blurted.

"What? You're kidding, aren't you?"

"Brad, trust me, I wish I was," was all I could utter. "It won't be bad, though. I promise. Giving Mike the Trooper is the right thing to do, just bear with me."

Brad, not prone to emotionally outbursts unless he is weak with hunger, only glared back at me. I was thankful he had just finished a big breakfast. This was going to be fine.

Moments after Mike left, Brad and I headed out to the station wagon. It looked more like a tank that had taken a direct hit or two. I held my head down in order to avoid the glare being shot at me from Brad, who was staring in disbelief at the monstrosity sitting in our driveway.

"Pull up on the door when you close it," I called out cheerfully as he tugged at the door, which had once again dropped down on its rusted hinges.

"Oh my Lord," I murmured as I started up the engine. By now several inches of snow had accumulated and there seemed to be no end to the storm. As I slowly pulled away, the tires spun to grab hold of the ground. Brad, his eyes firmly locked on the scratched door of the glove compartment, folded his arms as he slid down in his seat. Fortunately, he was small for his age so keeping his head below window level was not a problem. For me, it required a little more slumping. Had anyone peered into the car, they would have thought I was prepping for a gyn exam using the foot pedals as stirrups as I tried to keep my head level with the top of the steering wheel. And away we went.

"I'll drop you off at the edge of the parking lot, if you'd like," I cheerfully continued.

"Uh-huh."

Since I was unable to see the road from my reclining position, I glanced regularly at the treetops that passed by the windows in order to keep tabs on where we were. *Okay, there's the Barber's evergreens, the Carter's maple. Now, bear ever so slightly to the left,* I told myself as we slowly inched our way along. Our street is a mile and a half long with our house at the very end. As it twists and turns through the neighborhood, there is a hill located directly at the road's mid-point. A hill so subtle you're hardly aware of it unless you are riding a bike or walking with a bum heart – or driving in a raging snowstorm. As I approached it this day it seemed like a mountain looming up in front of the windshield. I sat up, if ever so slightly.

"Whoa, how are we going to get up this thing?" I murmured to myself, knowing Brad was not in much of a chitchat mood. It almost seemed a shame to add ruts to the clean white snow that covered the hillside but Mike assured me his car was capable of handling even the worst of conditions. With a slight curve to the hill, I decided this maneuver called for drastic measures. I sat up. I decided to gun it. As I grasped the steering wheel, my foot plunged down on the gas pedal. After a few spins of the tires we lurched forward, onward and upward. We seemed to make slow, steady progress at first, and as the two front tires crested the hill, I thought we were in the clear. However, the two back tires just didn't seem to want to cooperate. As the front of the car pulled and pulled, the back wheels spun and spun, to no avail.

"We're not going to make it," I shouted. So I mustered all the knowledge and experience I acquired during the last seven years living in the deep South. I slammed on the brakes to give the car a momentary breather (a decision my backwoods-northern-Minnesota Mike later pointed out was a real boo-boo). Brad, too, decided to sit up, if only for a moment.

"What are you doing?"

"Don't have a clue. Don't have a clue, boy," was all I could mutter as I clutched the wheel.

It seemed a second try was in order, so I gunned it again, but this time the car revolted. Instead of moving forward, up and over the hill, it started to slide. And slide it did, back and down and sideways. We were out of control, prisoners in a rusted metal box of ugliness that was slowly sliding backwards and sideways down the hill, until we finally jerked to a stop, wedged in the snow bank on the opposite side of the street, the nose of the station wagon sticking out into the path of any unsuspecting person who at any moment could come over the crest of the hill.

"Do you REALIZE I was supposed to be at the movies TEN MINUTES AGO?" Brad shouted. Breakfast must have been wearing off.

"Stay calm. I'll get you there," I countered as I pumped the gas, desperately trying to coax a bit of cooperation out of the monster that was firmly wedged backwards and sideways in the snow.

"I think we have a problem."

"NO DUH!"

"You probably need to go home and try and get a hold of Molly." While that plan sounded logical, on paper it was clearly futile. Molly was no doubt sitting in her mom's mini-van in front of the cinema, convinced she had been stood up on her very first date. And after her mom had made the effort to go out in this weather, I was sure Brad and I had both earned a place on their sh - - lists.

"Look, go home, call Molly. I'm going to call the cops. We've got to get this car out of here." With that Brad jumped out, using as much physical exertion as he could to make sure I knew just how unhappy he was, which actually provided enough adrenaline to get the car door shut on the first slam. I trudged across the street, slipping and sliding on the slope leading up to the nearest house.

"It'll all be fine, you'll see. You'll laugh about this one day . . . I *promise*." I called out to Brad as he stomped his way down the middle of the street.

"Excuse me, sir, could I use your phone? I've got to call the police." I asked the stranger whose house overlooked the hill.

"Wow! What a place to be stuck. Is that yours?" he asked.

With that I snapped back to reality. I was now not only in full sight of people, I was claiming responsibility for the one thing I hated most in the world.

"Mine? Oh, gosh, no. That thing's not MINE, but I've got to get it out of there." A quick push of the 911 brought, "Police, Fire, Ambulance, What's your emergency?"

"Police. Someone's car is . . ." I began.

"Police . . . what's your emergency?"

"There's this car wedged in a snow bank. It's *not mine* but it's sticking out into the street. You've got to get it out."

"Ma'am, can you call AAA? We're so backed up here."

"Well, I could try, but if they can't come you guys have got to send help."

"Try them first, if they can't help, call us back," I was instructed.

"How can I help?" came the AAA voice. When I explained once again that while the car was *not mine*, but what I needed was . . . and again I was told the weather had everyone waiting. At best it would be over an hour before help could arrive. The police were my only option.

"You've really got to help." I begged the police dispatcher once again. "If anyone comes over this hill they'll surely hit this car."

"We'll have an officer come. What's the make and model of the car?"

I didn't have a clue.

"It's the ugliest piece of sh - - you have ever seen." I stated into the phone as I smiled over at the stranger whose kitchen I was occupying.

"Ma'am, I can't put that in the record."

"Oh, yes, you can. It's *not my car* and that's all I know. Besides it's true – *you* wouldn't be caught dead in this thing," I assured the voice on the other end of the line.

"How 'bout the color. What color is it?"

"Gray. It's ugly gray."

"Okay, ugly gray it is. We'll have an officer out shortly."

Things seemed to be falling into place. This was all going to be fine after all. I needed to get home to see how Brad was doing, and the stranger on the hill promised to call me as soon as an officer arrived. By now the snow had reached such a depth it was becoming harder and harder to walk. Moments after my arrival back at my house the phone rang.

"Mrs. Wilson, good news. A police officer is here and he agrees – the hill is real bad. He's calling a plow and they'll get the car out, plus they're going to salt the road. Call you back."

Again, moments passed and a second call came in from my reporter/neighbor at the scene.

"Mrs. Wilson, the plow just got here. The driver's talking with the cop. Looks like they've got a plan. Yeah, they're making sure no one comes over the hill. The plow's at the top of the hill. I think they're going to close the whole road ... wait ... the plow ... it can't seem to get over the top. OH, MY GOD, NOOO..."

"Hello? Hellooo! Is everything okay?"

"OH MY GOD, IT'S NOT GOING TO MAKE IT!"

"Are you talking to me? Say that again."

"IT'S SLIDING . . . BACKWARDS . . . THE *PLOW'S* SLIDING ... OH, NOOOO ... IT'S CROSSING THE STREET ... OH, *MY GOD*. IT HIT YOUR CAR, AND IT'S *STILL GOING!*"

"Could you repeat that? Did you say it *hit* the car? You know that car's not really mine ... "

"OH MY GOD, IT CRUSHED YOUR CAR ... THEY'RE WEDGED TOGETHER, THE PLOW AND YOUR *CAR!* THERE GOES THE STOP SIGN ... YOU SHOULD *SEE* THE FACE OF THE OFFICER.

YOUR CAR AND THE PLOW, THEY'RE IN A HEAP AT THE BOTTOM OF THE HILL!"

Howard Cosell was milquetoast compared to the blow by blow description that came through my phone's receiver – so much vivre, such emotion, such thrill! "It's not my car," was all I could whimper back to my neighbor friend who was himself now gasping for breath.

"Mrs. Wilson, I think you better get back over here."

It all seemed surreal. "Brad . . . dear, there's been an interesting turn of events," I called as I once again stepped out into the snowy cold. As I trudged through the snow, I kept reminding myself: *this is a problem – a sad, unfortunate problem. We are not ecstatic. No, we are not even happy. This officer will not be expecting a big hug and a kiss. Keep cool. Everything's going to be fine. REAL fine!*

As I once again arrived at the hill, Mike's car was being loaded onto the back of a tow truck. The passenger side had taken the brunt of the blow. The back passenger window was no longer there, offering a quick solution to the rusty door hinges. I consoled the officer who stood dazed next to the crumpled stop sign with a these-things-can-happen nod of sympathetic understanding. Inside of me, miniature Rudys were dancing the conga in joyful celebration. But there was still the issue of Mike. I wondered how he would accept the loss of his best friend.

"We're back! Wow, what a drive. Hey, where's my car?" Mike called out as he stepped into the kitchen.

"Your car? What makes you ask?" I started fishing for words.

"My car. It's not in the driveway where I left it. Where's my car?"

"Well," I started slowly as I looked past Mike at the preacher who also stood somewhat baffled. "It's sort of been in an accident."

"You've been in an *accident*!?" Mike burst out.

"Well, no . . . that's the interesting thing. Your *car's* been in an accident. I was home, right here in the kitchen as a matter of a fact."

"*You* weren't in an accident but my car was?" Mike cocked his head as he tried to guess where we were going with this. "Is there something you need to tell me?"

With that I proceeded to explain the sequence of events with as much of a straight face as I could muster.

"You know my car . . . it's blue, not gray," he muttered as he tried to focus on the fact that he was now car-less. He then stepped closer and wrapping his arms around me, he whispered, "Well, thank God you're all right. I couldn't stand it if anything happened to you." And that's when it happened. As I pulled in toward his arms the burden was released. The car was history, or so I thought, and now I was free to love this man who had come into my life. The story had a bright and cheery ending. This really must be love . . . or so I thought.

Hunk-A Hunk-A Burning Love

Your typical television commercial is nothing more than a mere annoyance, an interruption strategically timed to intrude the moment a point is made, or even worse, to coincide with a program's suspenseful climax. Just as it looks like the good guys don't stand a chance, the action stops, and we are asked to evaluate the absorbency of our toilet tissue. Put to good use, commercials can be used as a welcome opportunity to raid the refrigerator or answer the call of nature (hopefully with toilet tissue that meets the requisite standard). Producers and advertisers see commercials as something different: an opportunity to sell products or even garner headline recognition post Super Bowl Sunday. Yet one night, this relatively innocuous occurrence changed my life, squashed my hopes, and drove me into a well-warranted depression.

A woman appeared on the TV screen, standing next to a seemingly stranded pickup truck on a lonely stretch of desert road. Two passersby stopped to see if they could help this stranger in her plight, and suddenly found this down-home woman morphing into a hot babe. Pulling off her baseball cap and shaking her head in just the right way, she asked if these boys would mind taking a photo of her and her truck; she needed a souvenir commemorating the 200,000 miles that now registered on her odometer. A hot babe with a 200,000-mile pickup. Oh, no.

It was clear what message the manufacturer intended to send. Audiences all over America would be convinced that they, too, needed to purchase this vehicle that appeared in mint condition after 200,000 miles of driving, just like these perfect physical specimens who happened upon each other out on a barren desert road. Whether male or female, TV viewers would barely be able to contain their excitement, their determination to stand up and shout, "Yes! Yes! I will buy."

As I watched the screen, I knew this commercial was having just the opposite effect on Mike. I suspect it had something to do with the Minnesotan in him, or perhaps it was some type of male macho syndrome, but the call he heard was not "buy, buy," it was instead, "Oh, *yeah* . . . you think that's good? Watch this."

Weeks earlier, Mike's car had been sent off to what I believed was the dump – baby dreamland for cars that are no more – because there certainly wasn't anything salvageable left in that piece of junk. The town's insurance had classified it as totaled and accepted full responsibility, which wasn't surprising considering the town's snow plow had crushed it. What was surprising was the monstrosity actually held a book value, and a check for what seemed like an amazing amount of money had just arrived in the mail. The whole ugly episode was closed.

"You know it's only her side that's a little dinged..." Mike mumbled as he sat mesmerized by the TV commercial.

"Dinged? What are you talking about? Are you referring to that *thing*, that piece of junk? Are you *crazy*? Your car has been put out of its misery. Let it rest in peace," I implored.

"I'll betcha a little work and she'll be as good as new..." he continued, not even aware that I was part of this conversation.

Good as new? I couldn't imagine that thing had ever been new, and now *it* was a *she*. She? *It's a she*? A female? Well, *she-e-e's* gone... crushed and *paid for*!

"We are *happy,* Mike. We are not sad. Repeat after me: I am *happy*, H-A-P-P-Y, very happy indeed," I tried to reinforce as I patted his cheeks. The glassy look in Mike's eyes suggested he needed shock treatment to zap him back into the real world.

It was clear Mike was still pining for his best friend. *It* had taken on the female gender; *it* was being elevated to sainthood. I understood the effects of grief. It was a road he needed to travel, and for many, grieving over a loss meant seeking the help of a professional. Could that be an option?

"We need an appointment with the grief counselor. Yes, there's been a death . . . of sorts. Actually, if you want to get technical it could possibly qualify as a *murder*. Yes, that's it. A *gruesome* murder. Untimely . . . in that . . . it, ahhh, *she* should have been put out of her misery long before." I suspected most grief counselors would be willing to offer support for someone who had been devastated by a murder, but I wondered if it could be pulled off with carefully chosen words like my conversation with poison control years earlier when Sofe drank wax stripper.

I glanced over at Mike. This couldn't possibly be happening. He was dreaming of a reunion, a resurrection of sorts. Thanks to some random, poorly timed commercial, Mike convinced himself that he could bring the old girl back, and he could continue to drive her. Not just the 200,000 miles, which seemed within easy reach. No, he was going to drive *her* to the 300,000-mile mark and perhaps, dare he dream, even beyond?

And so it went. Mike called the shop where the car's crumpled body still remained, and after some negotiating, it was agreed the "big stuff" would be repaired. Excuse me, *her* big stuff. *She* was ba-a-a-a-ck! The car I hated more than anything was back and Mike was happy as a clam. Little did I know his happiness would be short-lived and it would only be a matter of weeks before *she* would be out of my life forever.

Police lights bounced off the trees that lined the side of the road, filling my Trooper with flashing light late one summer evening. Just as we turned a corner near my house a police car seemed to appear out of nowhere, signaling Mike to pull over.

"Hey, why are you getting pulled over? Did you do anything wrong?"

"I don't know. I don't think so," Mike shrugged as he steered the car to the curb.

"Hi. Isn't your name Mike?" the officer asked as he leaned in the window.

"Yeah. How do you know me?"

"My name's John. You know your car? I was the officer who responded when it got stuck in the snow."

"Hey, hi," I leaned over to see the stranger who a few months earlier had been elevated in my mind to hero status. This was starting to feel more like a reunion than a traffic stop.

"I thought that thing was history," the officer said.

You and me both, I thought.

"But I get a call tonight and sure enough, there it is again."

"What do you mean, you got a call?"

"Well, it seems there was this fire, and if we didn't get rid of that car in the snow . . . "

"Fire . . . FIRE?"

"Yeah, the fire must have started small, but by the time I got there it was raging. A real neighborhood draw. Thank goodness you parked in the street."

Whenever Mike visited, he always parked in the driveway directly in front of the garage, but this afternoon a fresh load of mulch had been delivered and a mountain of wood chips kept him from his usual spot. Without a second thought he had left his car on the street.

Not wanting to get my hopes up once again, I hesitated to ask, "Was it bad?"

"Unbelievable."

"*Unbelievable?* You mean it?"

"Yeah, unbelievable."

It was too good to be true. Like a marshmallow that had surpassed a licking by the flames, this baby had fallen right onto the coals – windows had burst, shards of glass were everywhere, tires had exploded one by one, the entire front dash had melted into a pool of black smelly goo on the charred remains of what had been a floor. The destruction was complete, and Mike would never, could never, resurrect her again. Mike's saint of a car had been burned at the stake.

Poor dear, may she rest in peace.

Three's a Crowd

"Hey, wait! Come back," the nurse shouted as she ran out into the parking lot.

"But you just told us to go. Pleease, I wanna go home." My knees started to buckle. Dropping to the ground, curling into a little ball and crying blubbering sobs, the kind that produce streams of sticky nose-goo and red, puffy eyes seemed like a good option right about now. I was tired. I was cranky.

One month earlier, on Christmas Day, flu-like symptoms had invaded my body, and their grip was taking a toll in strength, maturity, and respectability. After being pickled in antibiotics for four weeks to no avail, I finally had been referred to a cardiologist who agreed to see me after hours on a cold and blustery Friday night. An echo test would confirm if I was not even dealing with the flu but rather bacteria in my heart. I no longer wanted to play this game called *Living Life as a Mature Sophisticated Grown-Up*. I no longer wanted to play this game called *Living*.

"The doctor needs to talk to you."

Uh-oh. Even outside in the dark of night I didn't like the look in the nurse's eyes. Doctors never stay late on Friday nights. They never send their nurses running out into freezing cold parking lots to retrieve patients unless the poor unsuspecting soul needed to be informed that a gruesome and untimely death was imminent.

"We've got good news and bad news," the doctor started slowly as he sat alongside Mike and me in the empty waiting room.

"The good news is we now know what's wrong with you. The bad news is you're not going home, you're going straight to the hospital."

If I'd had any strength left I would have jumped up and shouted, "I *TOLD* YOU SO. I *KNEW* I WAS DYING BUT OOHH NOOOO. YOU PEOPLE TELL ME, 'JUST SUCK IT UP, SPORT, AND THIS TOOO WILL PASS AND OH, BY THE WAY, CARE FOR ANOTHER HIT OF ANTIBIOTICS?'"

"You have endocarditis. You need to be in a hospital."

Endocarditis? The word sent chills up my spine. Twenty-two years earlier, as I had been released from Adonis-doc's care, he sat me down to enlighten me on the facts of a heart infection called endocarditis: *"If* you live and that's *if* we can cure you, your heart will be all chewed up by the bacteria. And *if* you live, *if* we cure you, you will probably need open-heart surgery to repair all the damage done to your heart, *if* you live, *if* we can cure you." If.

Go straight to the hospital? Brad and Darah were now deeply entrenched in their teenage years, so there was a strong possibility I could check into a hospital and they wouldn't even notice I was missing. But what if they ever found out that Mom was no longer vegging under a mountain of covers in her room but rather at death's door in the hospital? No, they needed to be told in person. A quick negotiation, not unlike when you buy a used car *(Hey, look . . . forgive that little squeal in the engine and I'll throw in a set of dice autographed by none other than the King himself),* earned me a quick trip home to tell the kids that Mom was sicker than anyone had guessed. The only bright spot in this evening was the fact that the cardiologist who happened to stay late and was now randomly assigned to my care was as cute as a button.

Because the hospital was technically full, the only way to be admitted was through the ER. Since it was a typical mid-winter Friday night at a big city hospital, or at least as big as Rhode Island is capable of producing, life was chaotic. A nurse who looked like she had spent way too many hours in this M.A.S.H. unit instructed me to maintain a holding pattern in a royal blue pressed plastic chair that was squeezed into a sea of chairs and vending machines in the ER waiting room. I needed to wait until someone croaked or was discharged before I could be assigned a bed. Since patients who leave hospitals without the requisite toe tag and body bag typically leave during daylight hours, it made more sense to pray for a croaking. In the meantime, I had the benefit of breathing in all the germs that were hanging heavy in the air from the dozens of patients, families, and friends who were also assigned a holding pattern. And hospitals wonder why infections run rampant within their walls!

Just as the blue plastic was beginning to lose some of its chill, and my ribs were beginning to numb from the pain of trying to make a nest out of its unforgiving shape, Dr. Shurman, my new doc, strolled in to check and see how things were going.

"Go home. This is no place for you to spend the night. We'll get you in tomorrow," he instructed. I made a mental note: never ever, *ever* again agree to visit an ER unless the following criteria are met (a) a cervix the size of a manhole cover as a result of being in end-stage labor, a prospect that seemed doubtful; (b) blood and guts oozing from multiple body parts as a result of some horrific trauma – a single body part oozing blood and guts would only call for the use of a Band-Aid; or (c) a bullet lodged somewhere deep in my gut. A bullet in a peripheral limb? Live with it. After all, how bad can it be? A knife in the eye would probably also qualify for consideration for a visit to an ER.

The next day did bring a hospital bed of my very own but I quickly suspected the reason for its vacancy: the patient before me, losing her mind, must have pinched the tube of her own respirator, resulting in sudden, unexplained, blissful death.

Filled with four beds rather than the two it had been designed to hold, my room was the very last at the end of a long winding hallway. A peanut-sized lady occupied the bed closest to the door. Quiet, unobtrusive, and minding her own business (as is typical of most comatose people), the first lady was a clear favorite for winning the Good Roommate Award. But then the other two patients offset her quiet demeanor in spades.

"Edith, you stupid little sh - -, it's about *time* you got here," screamed the lady from the far bed as soon as the nurse and I stepped into the room.

"Now, *Alba*, this isn't Edith, it's your new roommate," the nurse shouted back with a smile. Then, with the same smile plastered over her face, the nurse leaned over to me and whispered "Alzheimer's," which was supposed to make me feel better knowing that the patient, who seemed perfectly ready, willing, and able to kill me, was also crazy out of her mind.

"Who's Edith?" I inquired as long as I was going to be confused with this person.

"She's Alba's daughter. Doesn't come by much."

"Oh, no? What a surprise."

"Oh, just give Alba some time; she'll settle down." Initially I took this as good news. However, as the day progressed I realized that the nurse was probably saying *Give Alba another year or two and Alzheimer's will take her to a quieter place.* The screams got louder and louder as Alba switched back and forth from raging in my direction to spewing obscenities for the benefit of the nurses, who were by now easily a quarter of a mile down the corridor, hiding at their station.

The fourth lady, Madeline, was oblivious to Alba's screams as she studied the floor tiles while frantically pacing back and forth among the tightly packed beds. "It's hot. So hot," she would mumble down at the tiles. "I'm so hot." And with that Madeline started pulling on the strings of her hospital gown to seek some relief from her imaginary heat wave.

"Edith, get me the f - - - outta here. NOW! Do you hear me? You no good sh - -," Alba raged. "NURSE, NUUURSE...!!!"

The only hope in finding some relief was the flimsy curtain which hung from hooks in the ceiling. This prospect quickly showed the same promise as warming the North Atlantic with a single match. As a test, I pulled on the curtain, thinking out-of-sight, out-of-mind for dear, already-out-of-her-mind Alba. It was then that I noticed Madeline had made significant progress in disrobing. Her hospital gown hung precariously low off her elbows and at any moment was sure to lie in a heap across her best friend, the tiles.

Two o'clock signaled the arrival of visiting hours, which, not surprisingly, produced no Edith but did in fact produce 23 of Madeline's closest relatives, who were able to escort her back to bed and respectable decency. Daughters, sons-in-law, grandchildren, nieces, and nephews all filed into a room that could barely contain a doctor and a nurse at the same time. Medical people of any kind were out of the question, which I assumed they were just as happy about. Two of the high school-age granddaughters brought their boyfriends along. "Care to spend Saturday down at the hospital watching Granny strip?" "Hey, yeah, sure beats touch football with the guys."

One of the boyfriends seemed to fit right in, perfectly content standing around an old woman's hospital bed while the other kid's bulging eyes kept darting around, looking for something to crawl under. I glared at him, giving him the clear message that my curtained cubicle was off limits.

"Eat, Mamma, eat," Madeline was coaxed by her two daughters, who clearly headed up the group. Someone had brought a Tupperware filled with baklava. Eating seemed to be a sign for these people that Mamma was not only well but would be back home in no time, doing her daily tasks at her cheery best. Mamma Madeline, angry that her journey around the room to a cooler place had been interrupted by these loud and energetic people, was ticked. She slumped down in her bed, arms crossed, determined not to open her mouth for either food or conversation.

After what seemed like an eternity, the dinging of a bell finally signaled that visiting hours were over. Madeline's family dutifully filed one by one out of the room, and Alba, hoarse from spending the afternoon screaming at all the strangers, decided that throwing things offered another effective outlet for her emotions. Since my bed was not in a direct path from hers I was okay with that plan, too.

Most new days arrive as a dawning. One opens one's eyes, and as slumber washes away, thoughts, sights, and smells begin to fill one's senses. That is, after one has languished in sleep, whether for minutes or hours. When one spends a night in a crazy-looney bin tucked away at the end of a hospital corridor, no day dawns, it just melts into one long continuation of hours of uninterrupted insanity. Sunday had arrived.

After Alba had thrown everything she could get her hands on, she decided to branch out to larger items like chairs and IV poles. This adventuresome attitude was brought to a screeching halt when the nurses tied her arms to the bed rails, which was really, *really* not well received. Alba was only a touch miffed before she lost her mobility. Now she launched into a new tirade of curses and obscenities that could put a felon (not an ordinary felon, mind you, rather a felon with a *very* bad attitude and long criminal record) to shame. And when she couldn't think of a curse word, she'd resort to howling and screaming just for the heck of it, not unlike a baby who has just discovered it has a voice.

Survival mode kicked in. Two requisite means of beating endocarditis is to be infused with gallons of IV antibiotics and to get tons of sleep. I decided a cave needed to be built since my curtained cubicle offered no help in separating me from the chaos. I wanted to live. I needed to hide. I needed a place where I could plot my revenge against this evil villain named Edith who continued to be the brunt of Alba's anger. It became clear, the only way for me to live was for Edith to die.

My comatose roomie, cushioned with pillows around her motionless body, provided the best and easiest source of building supplies for my cave. Then, just as I slipped out of bed and into my sponge slippers with IV pole in hand, I caught a glimpse of myself in the mirror. What was I doing? Who had I become?

I was beginning to bear a strange resemblance to my even stranger roommates. I needed to get a grip. I could deal with this.

Madeline once again decided that temperatures had soared, and the best possible relief was to disrobe. As she paced the room trying to find comfort in the tiles, her threadbare hospital gown, which hardly covered the essentials, became too much for her to bear. So off it came. As I watched from under my paltry cave consisting of my own two pillows strategically laid over the bed, all I could mutter was, "Oh, well . . . go for it, girl . . ."

Eventually, a nurse making rounds noticed Madeline cruising the room, naked as a jaybird.

"There, there, Madeline, isn't that better? We don't want to walk around naked, now do we?" the nurse cooed as she helped her get dressed.

Are you kidding? This woman wants a hosing down with Arctic water, I mumbled to myself in my cave.

"Hey, when she gets like that again, give us a buzz at the front desk, okay?" the nurse called out, loud enough to be heard over Alba's screams.

Me? Keep an eye out for a naked Madeline? Sure, why not. Beats sleeping, and why would anyone think sleep has a place in a hospital? I mean, after all, who'd be so silly as to think a patient battling a heart infection could use a little shut-eye?

With that the nurse left, with only a glance in Alba's direction, setting off the next tirade of thrashes and rants, and suddenly, a ker-thunk and an "AAAGGHH" which was followed by a muffled "mm-mmmm." I looked over toward Alba's bed, something I had sworn I would never do, and sure enough, Alba was gone. Missing. Alba was no more. Pulling on my IV pole to get a better look, I scanned the opposite side of her bed. Alba lay sandwiched between the mattress and the bed rails, encased in a cocoon of bed sheets. Her sounds for the first time were muffled, and what a beautiful sound it was.

A fight ensued in my mind: *Leave her. Pretend you didn't know. God knows Madeline won't tell. Maybe no one will notice. No, she can't possibly be comfortable . . . Comfortable? Who cares about comfortable? Buzz the nurse, I'm sure it says somewhere in some medical journal that this isn't acceptable medical practice. But aren't there papoose things that hold patients in? That cocoon sure could be described as a papoose . . .*

Alba's trapping between the mattress and the rails was a double bonus since it also functioned as a muzzle. But, alas, compassion somehow reared its ugly head and, before I knew it, I was buzzing the nurse to come and bring Alba back into the scene. As good timing would have it, by the time the nurse made it down the hall to rescue Alba, Madeline had also reached full-birthday-suit mode, which killed two buzzings with one visit.

Visiting hours again. Madeline's clan marched in right on cue, this time bearing a kettle of soup. One might suspect they had camped out on the front lawn of the hospital. Had anyone strolled by, they would have sworn we were in the throes of a family festival, with "Oompah" being replaced by shouts from Alba's foul mouth.

Brad and Darah had been instructed that under NO circumstance were they to come and visit. "Tell them I'm contagious, tell them it's against hospital policy. Tell them *anything*, just make sure they don't witness this craziness," I pleaded with Mike, who himself had been coming later and leaving earlier than one might expect of a loving husband. It never occurred to me that this message needed to be spread to everyone I knew. Sure enough, in the early afternoon, Ginny and Nancy, friends who I count as some of my dearest, arrived unannounced.

"Hey, how's it going?" Ginny started as she stepped into the room. "Hey . . . ahhh . . . what the . . . " Looking around at the chaos, you'd swear my two friends had just been caught on Candid Camera. Was this some kind of joke? All I could do was shrug. Nancy, a gentle, soft-spoken lady, was already trying to crouch behind Ginny.

"Well, it's been great . . . we're thinking of you. . . ." And with that, they both turned and high-tailed it out the door, mumbling something about forgetting that this had been the very day they had scheduled a much-needed defrosting of their refrigerators.

Next to arrive: a woman, tall and distinguished-looking. She slowly wound her way through the crowd and then stopped at bed next to the window. Looking down at Alba, she whispered, "Hello, Mother." Edith. Edith in the flesh. The woman whose slow and torturous death I had been plotting the last 24 hours.

"NURSE. NUUURSE . . ." Alba screeched.

Okay Alba, now's your chance. Get her. Get her good, I thought. But Alba made no connection, not even noticing the woman standing over her, she continued to scream for the nurse. Three minutes later give or take a few seconds, and Edith's visit was over. She turned and walked out in the same deliberate manner as she had walked in. Edith was clearly encased in some sort of protective cocoon to lessen the pain of knowing what her mother had become.

As the day wore on I made promises to myself. Tonight will be better. Tonight Alba will realize what a pleasant stay she's having at the hospital and Madeline will lie quietly in her bed, admiring the lovely, stylish gown she wore. Tonight things will quiet down.

When the bell signaled the end of visiting hours, Madeline's entourage dutifully filed out the door. Then, within the half-hour a nurse came by to take a peek at her charges before the end of her shift. One look at Madeline and she went scurrying to get a doctor. Several medical people hurried back, all congregating around Madeline's bed. She had stopped trying to strip and I was half tempted to interrupt the doctor's powwow to tell them that this was a *good* thing. But something had happened. Madeline was taking a turn for the worse and I finally heard the medical people suggest her family needed to be called. *Called? Called to come back? They just left. They're probably just barely pulling into the garage as you speak and you want them to come back? Isn't it past visiting hours? So Madeline's doing poorly, so she may even die. Can't you guys just send the family a postcard, a sympathy note?* Knowing my input was probably not what these medical people were looking for, I just buried myself further down in my cave.

Madeline's family did not just come back after being called. They were practically airborne as they converged on what looked more and more like a dear departing matriarch. Picking up a few additional people along the way, they now spilled out into the hallway. Alba was ticked. Doctors and nurses continued to shuffle in and around the family, trying to administer whatever medical people administer when someone is dying. Instead of getting better, it was clear that things were only getting worse.

As the clock ticked past midnight, I decided I needed a plan. Not a coping plan, it was now time for an escape plan. There had to be some quiet place somewhere deep in the bowels of this institution where I and my IV pole could hide. I wasn't fussy. I just needed a place that was dark and quiet. Even sleeping standing up wasn't going to be a problem.

So I donned my sponge slippers, pulled my robe over my shoulders, and with IV pole in hand, shuffled quietly past the docs, Madeline's family, and even the boyfriend whose eyes were still bulging, which was not surprising considering he was now witness to a croaking.

I slowly shuffled down the hall, past neighboring rooms filled with patients who were by now deep in quiet, restful sleep. I took on the appearance of a lone refugee determined to move on to the safety of a foreign land. I shuffled past the nurses' station, making sure not to make eye contact. I needed to get far away, to a place where I wouldn't be recognized as that patient who escaped Room 1202. I contemplated a journey all the way home to the luxury of my very own bed. All I needed was my IV pole, but I decided against that after realizing at the current speed, I wouldn't arrive at my destination until sometime late in the summer, and as luck would have it, someone was bound to notice a tattered woman, pink robe slung over her shoulders, trudging alongside the roadway.

Finally after rounding a bank of elevators I noticed a lounge of sorts. Dark and filled with vinyl couches, it seemed to call out to me. *Come to me . . . who cares if I'm a tad cold and my edges are cracked. I'm dark. I'm quiet. Come rest in my arms.* This seemed as good as any place to hide.

Curling up on the couch, using my robe as a cover, I fell quickly into deep, blissful sleep. Madeline and Alba would never find me here.

"Can I help you?"

"Please don't tell. Don't make me go back. I just want to sleep." I pleaded to the voice that was standing over me.

"Can I help you? What are you doing here?" the man continued.

"Listen, let's just keep this between you and me. *Pleease* let me stay here," I begged, but then it dawned on me that if I wasn't careful, I might find myself escorted off to a psych ward that I was sure had some of its own Albas and Madelines.

The man, who was clearly perplexed but not especially mad, turned and left, but only minutes later another person showed up. The Head Nurse. Oh, no. I'd been tattled on. I needed to admit who I was and where I belonged, knowing that a quick peek at the bracelet that dangled from my wrist would turn me in. This person was kind, too, and rather than grabbing me under the arm and whisking me back to my room, IV pole dragging behind me, she said she'd see how she could help. It seems my room had developed quite a reputation for itself. With that, the man, who was also a nurse, arrived with a pillow and blanket as a show that I was not in trouble as I had feared.

A short time later, I was once again awakened, this time to be escorted to my own private room, a room that would remain my very own until I was released one week later.

"You know," the Head Nurse commented as she walked me toward my new room, "we would have made this change a lot sooner, if you'd only asked."

Emily

Dr. Shurman is a combo doctor: a little younger than Richard Gere, a little older than Josh Groban. Although he probably can't croon a melody like Josh, he has proven over time to be real smart. And smarts over singing ability is a good thing for a cardiologist. There is, however, a downside to the smarts – while these are the docs who know which course of treatment is best to fix you when you're sick, it rarely is "take two aspirin and get some rest."

I am a big fan of pills. Drinking anything for therapy or a cure is not a good idea because people in the pharmaceutical industry have extremely misguided ideas about what good tastes like. As a kid, I was forced to undergo an upper GI series of tests. I gagged, sobbed, and gagged for an entire afternoon while drinking the required goo, convincing the radiology technician that a career as a minesweeper or an Alaskan crab fisherman would be less stressful. Years later as I was preparing for open-heart surgery, another upper GI series was ordered. I was assured that "things were much improved." I was not to worry. I soon learned that adding a hint, a mere whisper, of citrus flavor to thick, chalky Elmer's Glue drink was some crazy medical person's idea of much improved.

I personally think everything should be fixed with a pill. I am even willing to tolerate the occasional stick of a needle as long as it is not administered by a med student or some nervous technician from the lab who's filling in on the night shift when a nurse or a phlebotomist cannot be found. What I do not like is tests, especially those tests that you clearly know the developers *never* allowed themselves to experience.

Dr. Shurman was smart enough to know of these tests. Shortly after I escaped the Wild Bunch in Room 1202 he suggested I undergo an echo test, of sorts. A normal echo test consists of lying on one's side while a technician covers your chest with goo and then runs a cold wand/microphone in swirly patterns all over you. A really skilled technician can chitchat at the same time he or she pushes all kinds of buttons on the surrounding computers. If you get a really rich cardiology practice, you will lie on a table with a center section that drops down, allowing the technician plenty of room to leisurely swirl away. And if you work real hard at forgetting that the numbers on the computer screens all around you could be spelling D-E-A-T-H, you can almost convince yourself you are floating on an inner tube in the pool of some exotic Caribbean resort. The only thing missing is the margaritas. Yes, a normal echo is one of those rare tests that could be considered a cakewalk.

But of course the high-tech pictures produced by a normal echo did not satisfy the medical community for long. It was just a matter of time before some sadistic person developed another variation, which causes medical people to salivate with excited anticipation over all the anatomical information it can reveal. You are *told* that in a trans-esophageal echo test a doctor gently inserts a flexible tube down your medicated throat to take pictures of the heart. In fact, it is a test in which your doctor rams a pipe the size of a garden hose down your medicated throat, if you think of *medicated* as sucking on a lozenge that melts into a syrup that tastes like urine with a hint of propane gas. (The pharmaceutical folks must have been having a real bad day when they came up with that one.) A Polaroid is stuck to the end of your garden hose (a.k.a. flexible tube) and apparently it provides medical people with exceptional pictures of the heart. I say, "mind your own damn business." After all, it is MY heart.

But Dr. Shurman was firm. He was hungry for information. Almost as soon as the test began I attempted to see just how fast I could escape until Dr. Shurman produced some kind of antidote to rid me of my uncooperative attitude. Some *wonderful* pharmaceutical person developed a drug that technically keeps you awake but totally zonked and happy. Just like in the ER, Dr. Shurman had redeemed himself. Richard Gere would have done nothing less.

After ten days in the hospital (four extra days being added to my stint to combat the bronchitis I must have picked up while hanging out in the ER), I was released. "Clear your calendar. I want you to rest," Dr. Shurman instructed as I headed home.

Rip Van Winkle was a light sleeper compared to an endocarditis patient. For most people six to eight hours of sleep is considered good. Even infants, famous for the amount of sleep they need, will at least wake regularly to scream for food and a clean diaper. Twelve hours of completely uninterrupted shut-eye and you're either a teenager or half dead. I was way beyond half dead. I was capable of keeping myself awake for only four hours out of every 24, and that was possible only through the aid of an alarm clock. The two times I did force myself to wake up were the afternoons, when my daily fix of IV antibiotics was strategically synchronized to the airing of the Oprah show, and again in the mornings for a brief visit to the kitchen to force down some food. Endocarditis proved to be a very effective weight-loss program.

After my one-month nap, an all clear was issued on the bacteria that had invaded my heart. It was now on to a slow and steady recovery. Or so I thought.

The dream was progressing steadily. The FBI were about to be called in, the parking garage was already surrounded. Then suddenly I turned and saw it – a tidal wave bearing down on me. Drowning me. I gulped for air. I was doomed.

I woke up with a start, happy to find it was all a dream. But as the vision of a tidal wave washed away into the recesses of my mind, the sensation of drowning did not. Sitting up, gasping for breath, I wondered why in the world I was still feeling the effects of a dream. There was gurgling in my chest. As I inhaled harder and deeper to bring fresh air to my lungs it was clear this wasn't just some awful dream. It was time to wake Mike and report a man overboard.

One of the downsides of being a chronic emotional lunatic is the crying wolf syndrome. The more lunacy you weave into your days on a regular basis, the less likely people who live with you will be willing to jump up in the middle of the night to throw you a life preserver. Some visible water on my side of the bed or the caw of a seagull would have made my announcement of a drowning much more believable. Yet, every time I tried to lie down the waves returned. Daylight brought relief but the next night the same tidal wave returned until I realized that sitting up tricked the waves into leaving me alone. So I slept in a chair.

"Doctor Shurman, an amazing thing happened the last two nights," I told him on the phone. "I drowned in bed."

"How soon can you get in?"

"In? You want me to make an appointment?" This was way too aggressive for my liking. I just wanted to chat. I wanted to be told, "Hey, no problem. Drowning is not a biggie. Take two aspirin and you'll be good as new in a jiffy." I didn't like the drop-everything-and get-your-butt-in-here attitude.

I consider myself a pretty good diagnostician, and just then what I needed was the Coast Guard, not a medical doctor. Of course, I've discovered a number of tumors over the years but so far none of them has progressed enough to convince any kind of doctor to do anything about them. And I did miss the mark once when I walked around for two weeks mumbling about a random ache in my gut. Convinced I had eaten a bad piece of shrimp, I expected nature to eventually take its course. But finally my very soft-spoken husband announced loud enough to suggest he meant business, "*Rudy*, shrimp does *not* stay with you for *two weeks*. Go to the doctor or I will take you there myself." Silly thing. Shrimp may not stay with *him* for two weeks, but if you take into consideration my bathroom issues, it could happen to me. But to placate my husband I did make an appointment with the doctor, only to find I had been walking around with a burst appendix. So. So I missed that one. So hold it against me. I was absolutely convinced that my drowning problems could be, if not talked away, at least eliminated with a carefully chosen pill.

Wrong again.

Only moments after a quick listen with the stethoscope, Dr. Shurman announced that I was in cardiac failure. Oh, please. Not that I wanted to butt in and tell Dr. Shurman his business, but if there's one thing I know it's words, and the word *failure* in the dictionary means "a state of inability to perform." The mere fact that I was sitting in his office chatting away would suggest that my heart was doing exactly what it was supposed to. I had lived enough years with voices whispering in my head *failure . . . failure . . . failure.* I know what a failure is and I was not about to just lie down and go along with this diagnosis because, other than the nightly drowning, I really felt quite chipper.

But Dr. Shurman was stubborn as smart people tend to be. He was not going to be swayed, and he even went so far as to suggest his understanding of my insides was a bit more on the money than mine was. So to prove his point he ordered another echo test. The normal kind, thank God.

Almost as soon as the echo was over a powwow was called. I was to meet with a whole team of heart people. Perhaps it was an effort by Dr. Shurman to bring in the troops for backup, knowing I was not going to be an easy one. Perhaps, as he suggested, it was to provide the most well-rounded medical expertise to oversee my quirky and very sick heart.

Open-heart surgery. Open-heart surgery Number 2. It seemed endocarditis bacteria buggies had been chewing on my heart months earlier, and this, combined with years of wear and tear, meant I needed not one but two of my valves replaced. At the same time, I was told any necessary housekeeping would be performed once the surgeon was "inside." And Dr. Shurman knew just the guy to do it. Dr. Aron Sing.

"Is he cute?" seemed a good first question to ask the group that filled my examining room. And with that the room fell silent. Dead silent.

Dr. Shurman – clearly the ringleader – was the first to pipe in, "Rudy, I think I know you pretty well, and you will just *love* this guy, trust me."

"Oh, yes, yes, you'll just *love* this guy," everyone in the room echoed, smiling as if some sort of impasse had just been hurdled.

"Okay, then, if I were your wife would this still be the guy to operate?"

"Absolutely."

"Okay, why don't we set an appointment for sometime in September," I suggested.

"September?"

Three months seemed accommodating; summer had just arrived; there were parties and several trips on the agenda, including an annual pilgrimage Mike and I made to the slums of Mexico. While other people spent their summers relaxing at beaches, Mike and I would gather a pack of whacko teenagers who were eager to hone their building skills or at least were willing to spend a week doing something over the top by building a house for a homeless family. Mike was the brains of the operation. I got to go along and hang out under the guise of chaperone.

"Rudy, you don't seem to understand," Dr. Shurman interrupted. "You can't be in a pressurized airplane cabin."

My extremely smart doctor was suggesting an implosion if I were to do something as simple as board an airplane. It was time to get serious. This was not going to go away. I made a mental note to schedule a good old-fashioned sob fest.

"You're sure this surgeon is a good one?" I stammered, hoping that the sobbing would not start before

I could get back to the privacy of my own home, surrounded by my highly intuitive and endearing pets.

"The best."

Sold. This surgeon would still be subject to a background and reference check prior his doing any slicing and dicing, but at this point at least he was starting out with very high marks. It was becoming clear my options were limited to (a) do this and take a chance at a longer life, or (b) die. An appointment was made.

In the meantime I was scheduled for a cardiac catheterization. A test that appears grizzly on paper is, with the right mix of happy drugs, not even a close second to the torment that can reign in a dentist's chair. I was assigned to a cardiologist known as *the cath guy*. He was a gentle doctor who, like his peers, was another looker, leading to my suspicion that buried deep within the Application for Employment used by my cardiologist's practice was the question, "Which stud/hot babe, living or dead, do you most resemble?"

As information was being gathered and the consultation with my new surgeon was fast approaching, I was instructed to bring along a trusted companion. I suspected the reason for this requirement was that after the gruesome facts of the upcoming surgery were laid out, most patients would be much more focused on thoughts of suicide rather than the rules of the road during the ride home. The obvious first choice for such a companion was Mike since, as a husband, he had already declared to God and man that he'd be there for better or worse (this being one of those worse times we hope will never happen but invariably do). But Mike was in the Mexican slums with his brood of teens, so I was forced to find another partner. Not wanting to turn this trip into a bummer, I decided this called for the services of a whacko. Mary was clearly the best whacko I knew. A kindergarten teacher who pales in maturity compared to her 5-year-old charges, Mary is never EVER without a laugh. This qualified her over other family and friends who might actually think serious thoughts while contemplating open-heart surgery Number 2. Mary saw her role as surrogate significant other as a hoot, which was exactly what I needed.

As soon as my significant other and I arrived for our scheduled appointment, Mary detected a shared Irish heritage with the woman who sat behind the reception desk. This caused Mary to launch into a series of Irish jokes, leaving Janice, the office manager, howling and me, the non-Irish heart patient who happened to be in full cardiac failure, panting for breath. Not to be outdone, Janice offered her own Irish jokes. Only after that category was thoroughly exhausted did our happy threesome move on to other shared topics such as menopause and, a universal favorite, men.

This caused other patients in surrounding waiting areas to look over with disdain; we were laughing in a place where, like a stone-cold cathedral in the midst of a funeral, laughter seemed utterly out of place.

Dr. Aron Sing in fact turned out to be Dr. Arun Singh. He arrived in his office at the scheduled time, whirling around with the intensity of a man who had places to go, people to see. Looney Tunes artists must have spent a day with this guy prior to developing the Tazmanian Devil character. Janice, clearly not a heart patient herself, kept one step ahead of this fast thinking, fast moving, highly sought specialist by handing out files, forms and phone messages as he whizzed by, all without losing focus on the current joke being shared by whacko Mary.

Dr. Singh's eyes sparkled, hinting at the wit that danced in his head, as he began to explain what lay in store. It became increasingly clear that I had connected with a good one. He held out a paperweight in which a mechanical heart valve was embedded. It looked like two metal doors swinging off hinges attached to a fuzzy white ring. This piece of apparatus, which would extend my life, looked more like it belonged inside a toilet rather than the human heart. But who was I to argue? As a repeat open-hearter, I didn't have any trouble getting to the heart of the matter, so to speak . . .

"Drugs. I want drugs."

"Don't worry, we're fully capable of managing pain," Dr. Singh assured.

"No, I want *way* more than managed pain. I want to be happy. I want to be really, really happy. And no respirator. I don't like respirators," I continued.

"Well, you will wake up on a respirator but we'll take it out as soon as you are able to breathe on your own." I made a mental note: fight the respirator (a really *stupid* plan I learned later, after my swollen face suggested that fighting a respirator is a loosing battle).

A date for the surgery was set, mid-week, far from any holiday or other distraction. The mandatory blood work and chest X-ray would be done at my leisure, if you can imagine any sense of leisure over the days leading up to major surgery.

"Report 6 a.m. the morning of your surgery, no eating or drinking after midnight," were my instructions.

"Don't I have to be admitted days ahead of time?"

"No, just show up that morning." This seemed way too casual. Where was the round-the-clock showering, the gallons of potassium followed by orange juice chasers, the days spent under the watchful eye of a team of medical specialists? In the name of cost containment, any careful monitoring prior to major surgery would have to be performed at home by my dog and two cats. I wondered if they'd be up to the task, knowing that unless treats were being distributed they were all sure to fall asleep on the job.

Surgery day finally arrived, and Mike and I drove in silence in the dark to the hospital. A good sign was that as soon as I stepped inside the hospital I became a part of a carefully planned and efficiently run system of processing patients. Nothing was left to chance, and it seemed only minutes passed before I was being wheeled up to surgery with Mike at my side. As the elevator stopped at the floor where the waiting room was located, quick good-byes were exchanged and he was gone. Next stop: surgery. A team of folks, ready and eager to perform their assigned tasks, converged as soon as the wheels of my gurney cleared the elevator door. Dr. Singh, his sparkling eyes peeking out from above his surgical mask, popped in to say 'hi.' There was no turning back now.

"Remember, drugs. I . . . I want lots of . . . of . . . d r u g s . . ."

The next thing I knew a swarm of nurses was doing their thing in Intensive Care. Too weak to move, too groggy to care, I just hung out, desperately trying to hold onto bits of conversation. Eavesdropping was the only activity available for me, and I wasn't going to let it get away. The guy on the gurney next to mine was having trouble. Internal bleeding; didn't look good. Being pickled in the very drugs I had demanded only hours earlier meant I would really have to concentrate to stay with the drama unfolding next to me. Had I not been so indisposed, I would have leaned up on my elbow and called over, "Your doctor, that wouldn't have been Dr. Singh, would it? No, of course not . . . Should have done your research, you might not be in this pickle right now." Like a dog rescued from the pound, there's no one more loyal to her doctor than a patient who has had major surgery and lives to tell about it.

The respirator's still there. Why don't these people take this stupid thing out?

"You've got fluid in your lungs. We're going to suction you and hopefully that will clear things enough for you to breathe," a voice whispered in my ear. I gave a thumbs up, signaling that whatever it took was fine by me. On one hand, suctioning makes the trans-esophageal echo seem like a summer picnic, but on the other hand it enables you to fill your lungs with fresh, clean air. Beautiful.

"What do you think you're doing?" No longer impaled on a respirator, but suffering the effects of my futile attempts to spit it out, I was only able to rasp to a resident who was heading over in my direction.

"Huh?" the startled resident asked. "I'm going to take a listen."

"Oh, no, you're not. I just watched you sneeze into your hand and then wipe it on a towel. You think you're coming anywhere near me? Get away from me before I scream bloody murder." With eyes bulging, this anonymous resident turned to the sink a few steps away and slowly scrubbed his hands, over and over and over, trying to wash off not only the germs but also the embarrassment, which I suspected was going to stay with him way longer than a few germs.

The word finally came down – I had made enough progress to warrant a move to a step-down unit. I planned on applying the same verve with which I had fought commands to walk after my first surgery to campaign for endless strolls down the hall. Four days later I walked out the doors of the hospital.

My homecoming was quiet except for the very reason I was in the hospital in the first place. My new heart valves, which were metal doors (or rather, highly polished pyrolytic carbon leaflets), banged shut every time they were called to service, which was a lot considering they slammed shut with every beat of my heart. This produced a sound just like the ticking of a time bomb.

I was at a crossroads. Mike and the kids were also at a crossroads since, if everything was quiet, they could also hear me ticking. After the initial fascination wore off we could be grossed out or ticked off (figuratively speaking) or we could just choose to ignore the racket. Darah and Brad, being teenagers, just seemed to shrug off the fact that their mother now sounded like she had somehow swallowed a large clock. Mike, being ga-ga in love, didn't care, but he probably wouldn't have cared if I'd had a toilet plunger surgically implanted on my scalp. Besides, his being from Minnesota meant he was just plain nice. People from Minnesota are way too nice about things that really piss off people from other parts of the country, i.e. the New York area, my neck of the woods.

I found the whole thing creepy, which I promptly reported to Dr. Singh. He told me, "it'd be *really* creepy if you didn't hear ticking, because you'd be dead." Which I guessed was some sort of consolation.

Eventually the ticking provided a unique opportunity to mystify people. As I continued to improve, I found that the sound was amplified in certain places, most notably public restrooms. Once as two women did their thing in a highway rest stop bathroom, one of the women picked up on the strange sound that was coming from my chest and bouncing off the tiles.

"You hear that?" the lady asked her friend.

"Yeah, whaddya think it is?"

"Gee, sounds like a clock," I interjected as I approached a booth. They must have agreed because both women held their digital watches up to their ears. But if it wasn't a clock, what could it be? By the time the source of the ticking had completed her bathroom procedures, the two women were mapping out an all-encompassing hunt into every corner of the restroom. I just hoped they weren't planning on calling in bomb-sniffing dogs. Restroom Watch performed at its very best.

A second encounter came as I lounged in a pool alongside a lady who was 90 years old if she was a day. Feeling obligated to initiate small talk, I forced out a "nice day."

This caused the woman to grunt back, making it clear there wasn't much nice about anything as far as she was concerned. To convince me, she informed me that she had just had open-heart surgery.

"Oh, yeah? Cool. I just had my second open-heart surgery."

"Well *I* have an artificial valve in my heart," she continued.

"Yeah? Me, too. I have *two* fake valves!"

Then the lady hissed that she hated the sound of the ticking; kept her awake most nights; didn't think she'd ever get another night's sleep, which didn't seem all that horrible considering she was probably already at death's door from a purely statistical perspective. I suggested, "Why don't you try to redefine the sound. Reframe it as something uplifting rather than annoying, like the rhythmic beat of a drum, a drum sound that represents life for you." My own demeanor surprised me. I was beginning to sound more like those folks in Minnesota, but since I was talking to a New Yorker, the effect was futile.

The next recovery episode occurred one night as I was innocently chatting away with Mike. A quick turn to my right where Mike was sitting caused a thing to stab its way out of my gut. Something hard and pointy was inside me, desperately wanting to get out.

"What the . . . !" I had visions of Dr. Singh leaving his entire tool bag or perhaps merely a precision-sharpened knife inside me. And if Dr. Singh left something behind in my gut, what would have prevented a Kramer type from dropping a Junior Mint into my gut from the observation deck high above the surgical suite? Like some innocent victim of a stabbing, the most appropriate response seemed to raise my hands in surrender.

"Dr. Shurman, you won't believe this, Dr. Singh left something behind in my gut!" I screamed over the phone as soon as office hours commenced the next morning.

"What?"

"Something stabbed me, something sharp and pointy, something that really wants to come out," I gasped.

"Oh, that," my cardiologist calmly responded. I had heard there were subversive things going on behind the scenes of all manner of corporate operations, but I never imagined my precious doctors were a part of any scheme of deception. "That's your pacer wire." A pacer wire. A known entity was lurking in my gut and no one seemed to care. It sounded like a major panic was in order but Dr. Shurman didn't seem the least bit concerned.

"That wire is placed near your heart during surgery in case you need a quick zap after you're closed, and then when you're discharged it just gets snipped off at the surface of the skin."

"But I don't like it. It stabs me every time I turn to the right. I want it out."

"You want it out?" The suggestion seemed incredible except that my definition of getting it out was a quick visit to the office, where a medical person would just pull it out, the way natives pull leaches from open wounds in the bush. But what I wanted would have called for another surgery, more anesthesia, and the resultant risk and recovery. Dr. Shurman suggested I just get over it, and once again being smart was way more appropriate than being emotional.

Like the old lady with the mechanical valve, I had a choice to make. I could hate my pacer wire and diminish its stabs by refusing to ever again turn to the right or I could follow my doctor's advice. We needed to get along, my pacer wire and me. It needed to change from a hated thing to a new best friend. And how could you have a best friend without a way to refer to it, or rather, she? Emily. Enter Emily, my new best friend and confidant, which has turned out to be a good thing. Other than expressing her displeasure when I turn to the right, she hasn't turned out to be one of those high-maintenance friends.

"Hey, Mom, you're going to be on TV," Brad exclaimed as he examined the TV guide. A cable documentary on open-heart surgery was scheduled just weeks after my discharge. Peering through the lenses of a TV camera into someone's open gut would be as good as seeing your own, since most guts look about the same, I would assume.

The show opened with an explanation that scientists in Russia – Siberia to be exact – had developed a technique of performing open-heart surgery on patients after packing them in huge blocks of ice, which is readily available in Siberia and inexpensive to boot. This allows Russian surgeons to avoid the use of the heart-lung machine. Oxygen bubbles are generated by the heart-lung machine as blood is swirled around and then circulated back into the patient. As this re-oxygenated blood eventually makes its way to the patient's brain, brain cells can be killed off. Bubbles on the brain, so to speak. The show went on to explain that people who spend more than an hour on the heart-lung machine can experience noticeable loss of brain function. This was not good news to feed to my teenage son, who was looking for support for his theory that his mother was crazy-stupid. Brad and I both know that over the course of my lifetime, I have spent the better part of a day on a heart-lung machine, way beyond the recommended dose. And now my excuse – being menopausal on a very humid day – was blown.

Garbage Envy

The year was coming to a close. The air was crisp and cold. Normal routines were being replaced by all things Christmas. Smells, sights and sounds of good cheer filled the senses. It was a time when the calendar told us our thoughts and feelings should be filled with love and joy and celebration.

And then it happened. I jumped in my car to make a quick trip to the market. That simple activity was intended to provide milk for my coffee, not to expose raw, ugly feelings of jealousy and greed. In keeping with New England tradition, my neighbor was a person I couldn't describe if my life depended on it. And this stranger had, over the course of the night, hung not one, not two, but four exquisite, massive wreaths on the front of her home. They were beautiful. From the street, these Christmas accents looked six feet in diameter. Then, as if sheer size were not enough, each was crowned with a bright, bold, red bow. Not an ordinary, ho-hum bow. No, these bows stood out as if to announce to the neighborhood and the world: *Look at me! Just try to ignore my dazzling beauty. I am all that a bow can be!*

Massive in size, sharp, crisp, and dazzling to the eye. A hint of a lining, spun with what appeared to be pure gold, peeked through the folds of red, adding sparkle and class. Even from the street you could tell the sun would never fade these babies. Rain? Snow? Not to worry. It was clear nothing the weather could produce would diminish these beauties. I found myself staring at these consummate Christmas bows.

Then my eyes caught the Christmas display mounted on my own front door. Cheesy at best. My single wreath was adequate, perhaps, but the bow was bargain basement, super-sale, end-of-season reject for sure. Obviously this neighbor didn't shop where I shopped. I had never even seen bows comparable to the ones that hung on her home. Then the thought crossed my mind, *What if she MADE those bows*? Now she was not only a neighbor with exquisite taste, but she had an abundant budget and the talent of an artist to boot.

I wanted those bows. *And why couldn't I have those bows*? But, alas, despite my being a covetor, at least I am not a thief. So I spent the holidays licking my wounds each time I was forced to drive by my neighbor's house and look up at her big red bows.

Then a miracle happened. In mid-January, as I drove home late one night, I gasped. There in front of my neighbor's house were four huge wreaths just lying there sandwiched between her garbage cans. And the big red bows were still attached! The objects of my envy were waiting for the early morning pick-up by the trash man.

I whipped into my garage and ran into the house. Standing there in the hall was my solution – my 17-year-old son, Brad. I grabbed him by the collar and looked him square in the face.

"How bad do you want to eat?"

"Huh?" he stammered.

"Quick . . . don your darkest clothes – that hooded sweatshirt you've got and your black pants. Then tiptoe next door and get the bows that are on the trash heap." When Brad balked at my request I reinforced it with my standard line: "Remember, I carried you in my *womb* for *nine months* . . . and you *do* want to eat, don't you?"

The need to eat combined with the womb thing has motivated my son to do an incredible number of whacko things for me. So he shrugged and headed off to change clothes.

"Be careful," I cautioned as Brad, with his hood pulled tight around his face, slipped out into the darkness. "Move slowly. These people have those lights that turn on when they detect movement."

"OK, Mom. I gotcha. You want me to steal. Stealth stealing. My life of crime is about to begin. No problem," he called back as he disappeared into the darkness.

Mike, who had been sitting on the couch nearby just rolled his eyes, "Rudy, do we *really* need to do this?" Typical man – unable to truly comprehend the finer things in life, especially when the finer things in life lay on your neighbor's trash just waiting to be rescued and returned to their rightful place of glory.

As the minutes ticked by, I wondered how I would best use my new bows. Then suddenly Brad stepped onto the porch dragging four massive wreaths.

"What are you *doing*?" I squealed as he pulled them through the front door.

"What's the matter? You *told* me to go get the wreaths. And here they are! I stayed low so their lights didn't even go on."

"Do you see how large these things are? I didn't want the *wreaths*, I just wanted the *bows*."

Brad's look told me I was clearly stepping out of bounds by expecting him to cower on his belly in the dark while painstakingly detaching bows from some stranger's trash. It was time for me to appreciate that he even complied in the first place.

The wreaths were so large I couldn't even pick them up, but I quickly untwisted the wires, releasing the bows into my quivering hands. At last they were mine! The most beautiful Christmas bows in the world were mine! Then as I looked down at the floor where the wreaths filled my hallway, I realized I had a problem – what to do with these huge circles of evergreen?

"Just take 'em back," Mike suggested.

"Take them *back*? And risk a second chance at getting caught?" I squealed. "Brad?"

"No *waaay!*"

"Come to think of it, if we take them back, then she'll know! The wreaths won't have bows on, and she'll *know*. Nope. It's better if we hope she's got menopause, then she won't even remember throwing the wreaths out in the first place."

I suddenly gained a whole new appreciation for the difficulties of mop-up after a murder. You knock someone off and now you have a whole new issue to deal with – what do you do with the body? As I looked down at the wreaths, they surely weighed about as much as a body, and now I needed to dispose of the evidence of my coveting, my crime. Brad's crime.

So, in keeping with the murder/crime theme, I headed out to the garage and grabbed a small saw and some garden shears. Then with careful precision, I chopped and snipped four massive evergreen wreaths into tiny snippets that could then be carted to my compost pile. All under the cover of darkness.

It wasn't long before evergreen remnants began to fill my hall and kitchen. Eventually as garbage bags filled with evergreen began to rise all around me, I realized that, like a killer cleaning up blood, I would not be done without a major cleaning job to dispose of the evidence. But every time I began to grow weary, all I had to do was look at my new big, beautiful bows lying on my kitchen table.

"Hey, Mom," Brad quipped as I finally wiped up the last bit of greenery, "How are you ever going to hang these bows? As soon as you do, she'll *know*. Are we now going to have to move sometime before next Christmas?"

Not a problem – as Christmas arrived one year later, I proudly mounted one of my big, beautiful red bows on a wreath and hung it above the mantel of my fireplace. It had been quite a journey getting to here. My childhood dream of owning a fireplace had been fulfilled, and despite challenges along the way, life was grand.

Acknowledgments

This book would not have been possible without Mary Lhowe and Laura Hudson, my wonderful editors. Thank: You four, your wisdom and support while, helping Me, deal with, my comma problem;

To Karen Saunders of Macgraphics Services, Ann Marie Gordon of United Graphics, Joan Stewart, The Publicity Hound and April Williams of North Star Marketing and Promotion: When I went into this project I was blind and now I see. Thanks for all your help and support.

To Ginny Hudson, George Samuels, and Nancy Svendsen: Pigtails and pom-poms couldn't make you guys better cheerleaders. Whenever The Voices told me to quit, you were only an e-mail away.

To Sue and Neal Tompkins: They don't make better friends than you.

To the January Birthday Bunch: It's a privilege to join your ranks despite being an Aries and a Leo.

To my readers, Barbara Barber, Marge Rhody, Janice Raposa, Philip Lecky, and Anne Marie Petteruti: Your time and input are so very much appreciated.

To my incredible medical team that keep me going: Drs. Alan Shurman, Arun Singh, Fred Christian, Thomas Drew, Doreen Wiggins, and David Ashley. You guys are so good and so fun to work with, I'll never be able to move away unless you all agree to come with me.

To Graham Martin and Bob Petrucelli, The Numbers Guys: Do you have any clue where I'd be today without your support and expertise?

To the hip girls at Stonehill College: What a hoot! I'm only sorry you never let me come room with you.

To Judy Buch, Karen Hinds, and Carol Hamblet Adams: Thanks for helping me keep my focus on what's truly important.

To Cindy Zeigler: Thanks for giving me the scoop.

To the Wilsons: You produced one heck of a kid. He taught me how to believe in myself and dream big dreams. Sharing a meal with you and the Krupas is like getting front-row seats at the best comedy club in town.

To Omi, Chris, and the rest of the gang: I love you.

Quick Order Form

❏ YES, I want _____ copies of **Take Heart! True Stories of Life, Love, and Laughter** at $12.95 each, plus $4.00 shipping for the first book and $2.00 for each additional book. (Rhode Island residents please add 7 % sales tax.)

Name _____

Address _____

City/State/Zip _____

Phone (_____) _____

E-mail _____

Please charge my account:

Credit Card # _____ Exp. Date _____

Signature _____

Fax orders: 401-885-4058. Please send this form.

Telephone orders: Call 888-233-8960
Please have your credit card ready.

E-mail orders: info@Broadhorizonspress.com

Postal orders: Broad Horizons Press
P.O. Box 528
East Greenwich, RI 02818

Web site: www.rudywg.com